MUMMIES

Life after Death
in Ancient Egypt

By
Renate Germer

With contributions by
Hartwig Altenmüller,
Karl Heinz Höhne,
Hannelore Kischkewitz,
and Jens Klocke

Prestel   Munich · New York

This book has been published in conjunction with the exhibition "Mummies: Life after Death in Ancient Egypt" held at the Museum für Kunst und Gewerbe Hamburg (January 24 – April 20, 1997) and the Roemer- und Pelizaeus-Museum, Hildesheim (June 22 – November 30, 1997).

Edited by the Museum für Kunst und Gewerbe Hamburg

Support for the exhibition was generously provided by the Hamburgische Landesbank

Authors
Renate Germer
Hartwig Altenmüller (H.A.)
Karl Heinz Höhne (K.H.H.)
Hannelore Kischkewitz (H.K.)
Jens Klocke

Translated from the German by Fiona Elliott
Manuscript edited by Andrea P. A. Belloli, London

Front cover illustration: Coffin of Mutirdies (see illus. 3); linen wrapping from the mummy of a woman, Kestner-Museum, Hanover (see illus. 118–20)
Illustrations on double pages, see p. 143
For photography credits, see p. 143

Die Deutsche Bibliothek - CIP- Einheitsaufnahme
Mummies : life after death in ancient Egypt ; [in conjunction with the Exhibition "Mummies: Life after Death in Ancient Egypt" held at the Museum für Kunst und Gewerbe Hamburg (January 24 – April 20, 1997) and the Roemer- und Pelizaeus-Museum, Hildesheim (June 22 – November 30, 1997)] / by Renate Germer. With contributions by Hartwig Altenmüller ... [Ed. by the Museum für Kunst und Gewerbe, Hamburg. Transl. from the German by Fiona Elliott. Copy-ed. by Andrea P. A. Belloli]. - Munich ; New York : Prestel, 1997
Dt. Ausg. u. d. T.: Das Geheimnis der Mumien
ISBN 3-7913-1804-7
NE: Germer, Renate; Elliott, Fiona [Übers.]; Ausstellung Das Geheimnis der Mumien - Ewiges Leben am Nil <1997, Hamburg; Hildesheim>; Museum für Kunst und Gewerbe <Hamburg>

Prestel-Verlag, Mandlstrasse 26 · D-80802 Munich, Germany
Tel. (89) 381709-0; Fax (89) 381709-35
and 16 West 22nd Street, New York, NY 10010, USA
Tel. (212) 627-8199; Fax (212) 627-9866

Prestel books are available worldwide.
Please contact your nearest bookseller or write to either of the above addresses for information concerning your local distributor.

Designed by Petra Lüer
Offset lithography by Repro Line, Munich
Printed and bound by Offizin Paul Hartung Druck GmbH & Co. KG, Hamburg
Printed in Germany
ISBN 3-7913-1804-7 (English edition)
ISBN 3-7913-1782-2 (German edition)
Printed on acid-free paper

CONTENTS

FOREWORD

BOOKS, CATALOGUES AND EXHIBITIONS ON THE ART and culture of the wondrous lands along the River Nile are met with intense interest throughout the world, and there would seem to be no end in sight to this remarkable phenomenon. The enduring fascination of ancient Egypt is nurtured by the continuous flow of new, often spectacular research and archaeological finds.

Mummies: Life after Death in Ancient Egypt presents a picture of an area that is central to our understanding of Egypt and which itself consists of a whole range of individual considerations and issues. Since scholars first successfully deciphered Egyptian hieroglyphs over 170 years ago, temples and tombs, reliefs and wall-paintings have broken their silence of thousands of years and begun to 'talk' again. Nevertheless the mummies, the embalmed, linen-wrapped mortal remains of pharaohs, officials and priests, men and women, adults and children have only revealed their secrets with some reluctance. How was it that the Egyptians were able to preserve the bodies of their dead so that they have survived to this day practically unscathed? How did these people die and what had their lives been like? What lay behind the immense efforts the Egyptians made to prepare their deceased family members for the afterlife? These and many other questions are answered in this book, which largely owes its existence to the knowledge and scholarship of Renate Germer of the University of Hamburg.

With its many illustrations this book focuses in part on the protection and decoration of the mummies of ancient Egypt, which included finely crafted masks made from linen cartonnage or plaster, as well as mummy portraits, bead nets and, of course, magnificently painted coffins. In addition to this the dead were buried along with the implements needed for the ritual, magical reanimation of the mummy, while amulets, burial papyrus scrolls and various other items were also provided in order to protect the deceased on their journey into the realms of the dead and to ensure their continued existence in the afterlife.

This book, which accompanied the exhibition on mummies, 'Das Geheimnis der Mumien,' organised by Cornelia Ewigleben at the Museum für Kunst und Gewerbe in Hamburg and at the Roemer- und Pelizaeus-Museum in Hildesheim, also highlights the main aspects of this ancient culture that has intrigued so many Europeans since the 17th century. In those early days interest centred on the highly prized, finely ground powders that were derived from mummy remains and sold by apothecaries as medical remedies. During the Baroque age, mummies acquired status as precious exhibits in princely curiosity cabinets, and, in the 19th century, those who were in a position to do so would arrange the unwrapping of a mummy as a social event. It was this practice that led in the early 19th century to the beginnings of Egyptology as a field of study which now spans a period of over 1500 years - from the disappearance of thousands of years of Egyptian tradition in the dying days of the Roman Empire to our own, highly technological present.

Nowadays the new possibilities of virtual reality and computer-assisted medical diagnosis present us with an increasingly clear picture of living conditions in ancient Egypt. It is as though the lives and even the actual appearance of these mummified individuals are recreated and reconstructed before our very eyes. The days when the examination of a mummy in effect first entailed its destruction are finally over, for state-of-the-art X-ray techniques and computer scans now allow the interior of a mummy to be viewed without the need to open up its linen wrappings and or indeed even to touch that person who once lived in the Valley of the Nile.

Intensive research in recent decades has unlocked many of the secrets and solved many of the puzzles surrounding the mummies of ancient Egypt - but clearly this is work still in progress and will doubtless lead to yet further discoveries in the years to come.

Wilhelm Hornbostel
Museum für Kunst und Gewerbe Hamburg

Arne Eggebrecht
Roemer- und Pelizaeus-Museum, Hildesheim

I

THE MUMMY — A BODY FOR ETERNITY

EGYPT — THAT MYSTERIOUS LAND ALONG THE RIVER NILE — is as fascinating today as it has ever been. Thousands of years ago, the pharaohs' master builders created monumental structures which we still admire today. These include the pyramids at Giza; of the original seven wonders of the ancient world, they alone have survived. During the time of the pharaohs, religion was an immensely important part of Egyptian life, and there were numerous gods in human or animal form, with some combining features of both. In the lands of the eastern Mediterranean and in Mesopotamia, the scientists of ancient Egypt, above all the doctors, had the highest of reputations. And the embalmers of ancient Egypt were unequalled in the art of preventing the natural process of decay that normally overtakes the human body after death.

In our own highly technical world, where the subject of dying is largely avoided, seeing an ancient Egyptian mummy can be a strange experience. A whole range of emotions may be inspired by the sight of the preserved body of someone who died two or even three thousand years ago. Why did the Egyptians mummify their dead, and how was it done? There are no easy answers to these questions because, despite the

existence of Egyptology for a good 150 years now, and despite the application of the most modern of methods to mummy research, we are still only making gradual headway in our understanding of a people whose culture began in the valley of the Nile four thousand years before the birth of Christ and did not come to an end until the fifth century A.D.

The Egyptians left us large amounts of information about their religion in words and pictures on papyrus rolls as well as on the walls of temples and tombs. These tell us why they wanted to preserve the human body beyond death: it was their belief that there was an afterlife beyond this world which would last for all eternity, but which could only be entered if the deceased's body was intact and still able to function.

So it does initially seem contradictory that there was little or no reluctance to open the body and remove the viscera, even quite roughly. And it also seems puzzling that the embalming process was not depicted or described anywhere. Could it have been a secret process known only to initiates?

On the contrary, the explanation for the complete lack of texts or illustrations on the subject of embalming is perfectly straightforward. The fact is that the actual techniques of embalming were simply not considered important enough to be shown alongside the gods or representations of the afterlife, and they did not even merit a place amongst the scenes of daily life that feature in many tomb decorations.

When a person had died and their soul, the *ba,* had flown from the body in the form of a bird, there was only a soulless shell left behind. Only when all the stages of mummification had been completed did life

1   The coffin of Mutirdies, detail

(see illus. 3)

17

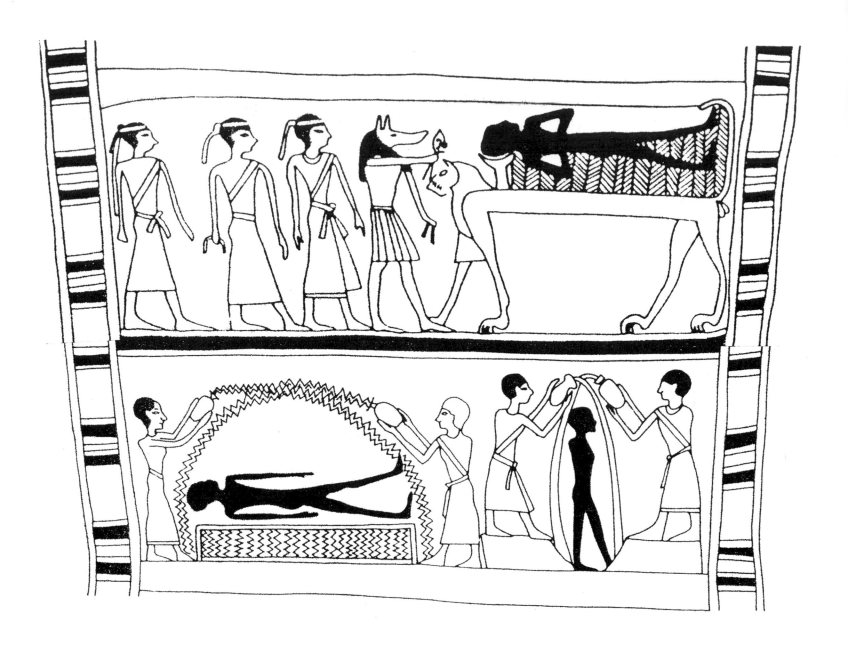

return to the body during the ceremony of the Opening of the Mouth, about which more will be said later. And everything that happened after that moment was of the utmost importance for the afterlife of the deceased.

In the past, certain tomb paintings were thought to be depictions of the mummification process, but thus clearly were misinterpreted, for they only show coffins being made. There are, however, a small number of coffins with decorations which do at least refer obliquely to the practice of embalming. These coffins were produced as a series to meet demand as it arose, and the names of the deceased were only added later. They date from the second and first centuries B.C. and were found in a family tomb in El-Hibe in Middle Egypt. As was customary, most of the decorations concern events after the mummy had been completed. On the outside of the lid of the coffin belonging to Mutirdies, six out of a total of eight sections of decoration show scenes from the afterlife, while the topmost scene and that at the foot of the lid show Osiris, the god of the

underworld, in a boat, a motif found on many other coffins which will be discussed in more detail later. Three of the scenes show priests in front of a richly laden offering table, while a fourth depicts the wrapped mummy lying on a lion-shaped bier, with four canopic jars placed under it. Above it, there is a small inscription with the name of the deceased. To the right of the bier, there is a group of priests carrying standards.

Two of these scenes are most unusual: the second and fourth from the foot of the lid. Similar scenes exist in an almost identical form on the coffin of Djedbastetiuefankh from this same family tomb, although there they occupy the two lowest sections on the lid. The scenes in question portray the black, naked corpse of the deceased, once recumbent and once upright, with two priests pouring purifying liquids over it. In the register above this, the deceased is shown lying on a lion-shaped bier. Below the body, there is a schematic depiction of new life in the plant world, to symbolise the regeneration of the deceased in the afterlife. Four priests, one wearing an Anubis mask, approach the bier.

3 The coffin of Mutirdies, 2nd-1st century B.C.
Painted wood, length: 170 cms.
From El-Hibe.
Pelizaeus-Museum, Hildesheim, Inv. 1953

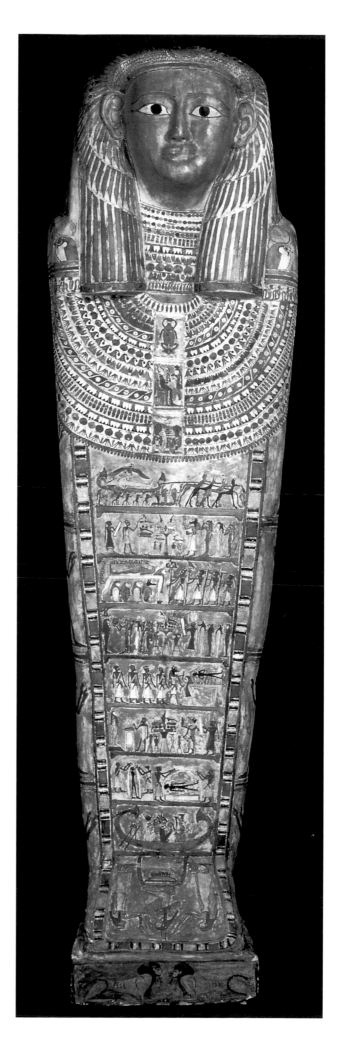

Interesting and unusual though these depictions on the coffins in
El-Hibe are, they nevertheless tell us little about mummification. And
although embalming rituals are described in two papyri from the end of
the first century B.C., these only refer to the embalming and wrapping
of individual parts of the body and give the relevant words to be recited
in the process. Unfortunately, these papyri neither constitute a hand-
book of the art of embalming nor divulge the techniques involved in
creating a mummy. It seems most likely that the skills required were
simply passed down from father to son, or from master to apprentice.

Herodotus, however, the Greek writer who travelled in Egypt in
the fifth century B.C., viewed the process of embalming with great
interest. He wanted to convey an idea of the special nature of that
country to his readers, and in this context mummification was worthy
of mention, with the result that it is only in his writing that we can find
an authentic account of the art of mummification in pharaonic Egypt.

7 Bitumen, container for embalming oils, bees wax and conifer resin
(all modern with the exception of the container).
Alabaster container 9.5 cms in height.
Museum für Kunst und Gewerbe, Hamburg, Inv. 1924.24

8 Three hooks for removing the brain during the embalming process, Late Period.
Bronze, length: 28 cms, 28.5 cms and 33.5 cms.
Rijksmuseum van Oudheden, Leiden, Inv. AB 140b, 140c, 140d

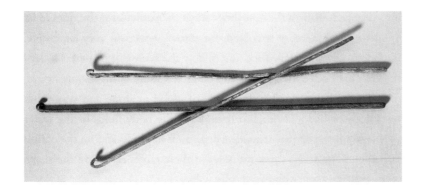

disposed of in a ditch away from the tomb. So we know that the tool used to remove brains was a bronze hook of up to 18 inches (40 centimetres) in length (see illus. 8). The bent end of the instrument that was inserted into the nose came in many different shapes, rolled up like a snail's shell or more like a needle. This hook was used to penetrate the ethmoid bone and open up a path into the brain. An alternative method which involved the brain being removed through the foramen magnum in the nape of the neck is not described by Herodotus although it was just as common.

After the brain had been removed, the embalmers poured embalming oils into the skull — the oils perhaps having first been heated to make them pour more easily. Inside the skull, the oils would then solidify and form a crust, as can be seen very clearly on computer tomography (CT) scans of various mummies (a form of X-rays). Chemical analysis of embalming oils has confirmed that these were indeed resinous, just as Herodotus described them. They consist mainly of conifer resins, including a certain amount of beeswax and oils perfumed with plant products, even bitumen in some cases (cf. illus. 7). Some of the ingredients had to be imported from abroad, such as conifer resins from the forest regions of the Lebanon and bitumen, a mineral-based asphalt, from the Dead Sea.

Next, Herodotus describes the removal of the bowels from the chest and abdominal cavities: '... they then with an Ethiopian stone make an incision in the side, through which they extract the intestines; these they cleanse thoroughly, washing them with palm wine, and afterwards covering them with pounded aromatics.' Herodotus does not report what happened then, but modern research into mummies and canopic jars has provided the answers. An incision into the wall of the abdomen opened up the way into the body so that the viscera could be removed. Only the heart, as the seat of all thinking and feeling, either remained in place or was returned to the chest cavity after mummification. The heart was frequently replaced with a heart scarab (see illus. 12 and 13), a kind of magical substitute heart, about which more will be said later. Next, the embalmers cleansed the viscera, treated them with natron, and wrapped them in linen. After this, each package was placed in its own canopic jar.

Herodotus goes on to detail two further processes, the refilling of the body after the removal of the organs and its preservation using natron, although he describes them in reverse order.

First of all, the body would be treated with natron — not in liquid form as was once assumed, but in dry form, filling the body and being packed around it. Natron is a mixture of sodium carbonate and sodium bicarbonate (see illus. 10). Being hygroscopic, it would draw the moisture from the tissues. This process of desiccation, which preserved the body and prevented decay, was helped by the very dry climate of Egypt. In some cases, the natron was placed in small linen bags, which had the advantage that as moisture was absorbed it was easier to replace the damp natron. This natron treatment lasted between thirty-five and forty days.

After the tissues had dried out, the embalmers would anoint the body with various embalming oils and pour more oils inside it — the same ones that had been used to fill the skull.

The last stage of the embalming process was the refilling of the chest and abdominal cavities with various materials. Most frequently used were linen or sawdust (see illus. 11). More rarely, silt from the River Nile

9   Stone knife, late 4th century B.C.
Flint, length: 6 x 21 cms.
From Abusir.
Kestner-Museum, Hanover,
Inv. 1921.2/28

10   Natron, loose and filled
into linen bags (modern)

11   Materials used for re-stuffing
bodily cavities: linen, sawdust,
Nile silt, onions and lichen

might be used. The two pharaonic mummies of Siptah and Ramesses IV are packed with an aromatic lichen known as tree moss (*Pseudevernia furfuracea*, L. Zopf). Since eyeballs, which consist largely of water, would shrink significantly during treatment, small linen pads would be laid into the eyesockets. Sometimes, small cooking onions might be used to replace them.

After the body of the deceased had been preserved, anointed, and refilled, the incision into the wall of the abdomen would be closed with a linen pad. The body was now prepared for eternity. But the Egyptians did not trust to the skills of their embalmers alone and spared no efforts to ensure that the mummy would also be protected by magic.

AMULETS — PROTECTION FOR THE MUMMY

AMULETS PLAYED AN IMPORTANT PART IN THE LIFE OF THE ancient Egyptians, who believed in them as protection from all known evils. They used to be worn on a cord or gold wire round the neck or wrist, or set in a ring. The belief was that this protection could equally well serve the dead, so mummies were given amulets to accompany them on their journey into the afterlife. The higher the social standing of the deceased, the more numerous and precious these amulets would be.

Certain amulets still in use in Roman times date back as far as the Old Kingdom — for example, the *wadjet* eye, which had its origins in the myth of the healing of the god Horus's injured eye. During the course of Egyptian history, the variety of amulets constantly increased, reaching a high point in the 26th Dynasty, when a body would often be

12/13   Heart scarab with inscribed base
(Spell 30B from *The Book of the Dead*),
c. 850 B.C.
Limestone, height: 2.4 cms, length: 8 cms.
Pelizaeus-Museum,
Hildesheim, Inv. 1246

14   Gold sheets to cover the eyes and
the tongue, Roman Period.
Gold plate, length: 3 cms and 2.5 cms.
Pelizaeus-Museum,
Hildesheim, LH 5, LH 6

15   *Ba*-bird, Late Period to Ptolemaic
Period. Gold plate, 2.2 x 3.7 cms.
Rijksmuseum van Oudheden, Leiden,
Inv. L.V. 63.

16   Nine finger caps,
4th-3rd century B.C.
Gold plate, length: c. 3.5 cms.
Pelizaeus-Museum, Hildesheim, LH 4

17   Two-finger amulet,
26th Dynasty. Stone, length: 9.1 cm.
Kestner-Museum, Hanover, Inv. 279

Opposite page
18   Amulets in shape of various symbols
and deities. Faience, height: 1.3-5.8 cms.
Museum für Kunst und Gewerbe,
Hamburg

positively covered in amulets as in the case of the Lübeck Apothecaries' Mummy (see illus. 105 and 106). Approximately three hundred different kinds have been recorded from this period, although some occur very infrequently.

Each individual amulet had its own protective powers and its own fixed place on the body of the mummy. Most were made of blue-green faience because green, symbolic of new growth, was thought of as the colour of regeneration. A much smaller number were made from fine semi-precious stones.

Only one kind of amulet was ever placed inside the body by the embalmers — the heart scarab. For the Egyptians, the heart was the seat of all thinking and feeling and, consequently, the source of an individual's identity. So the heart was either left inside the body during embalming or returned there after the removal of the organs. The heart — or the heart scarab in its place — would be needed at the final judgement to bear witness as to how the deceased had lived (see illus. 12 and 13) and, as part of the process, would be weighed against a statuette of the goddess of truth (Maat) under the gaze of Osiris, the god of the underworld. The scarab was the symbol of regeneration because of the way scarab beetles procreate. The male rolls a ball of dung much bigger than himself into which the female then lays an egg. Believing that it in fact regenerated itself inside the ball of dung, the Egyptian revered the scarab beetle as sacred. For them, it embodied the notion of the sun rising each day and therefore, by association, guaranteed the resurrection of the deceased by ensuring the favourable outcome of the final judgement. To this end, the underside of the scarab was usually inscribed with Spell 30B from *The Book of the Dead*, a collection of spells and

19 Amulets of deities.

Faïence, height: 4–7.9 cms.

Museum für Kunst und Gewerbe,

Hamburg

incantations, often accompanied by small drawings, that the deceased was thought to need in the afterlife. In this spell, the deceased implores the heart not to speak against him or her when it comes to the weighing ceremony:

> *O my heart which I had from my mother!*
> *O my heart which I had from my mother*
> *O my heart of my different ages!*
> *Do not stand up as a witness against me,*
> *Do not be opposed to me in the tribunal,*
> *Do not be hostile to me in the presence of the Keeper*
> *of the Balance.*

After the embalmers had refilled the chest and abdominal cavities with linen or sawdust, they would frequently cover the incision with a beeswax plate or with a two-finger amulet made out of black stone (see illus. 17). The function of these plates is not entirely clear, although they probably simply served to hold the two edges of the incision together.

Thin gold sheets were used to cover the eyes and mouth and encase the fingers and toes (see illus. 14 and 16). Gold was used to ensure that these body parts would all function again in the afterlife. This practice was originally reserved exclusively for royal mummies, as in the case of the only one preserved in its original state, that of Tutankhamun. Altogether, there were 143 objects secreted in amongst the linen wrappings round his body, each with its own particular magical protective function. It was not until the Late Period and particularly the Graeco-Roman period that gold was also used for non-royal mummies. Up until this point, non-royal mummies usually only had a small number of amulets in the form of a neck-chain, wristband, or ring.

From the 26th Dynasty onwards, amulets were mostly small in size and sewn onto the linen once the mummy had already been wrapped. They can be categorised in several large groups.

Opposite page

21 Faience amulets from a mummy including two triads of deities with Isis, Horus and Nephthys, a winged scarab, the four sons of Horus and two djed arrows, Ptolemaic Period. Faience, width of scarab: 21.3 cms, length of djed arrow: 9 cms.
Pelizaeus-Museum, Hildesheim, LH 19

20 Mummy wrapping with text from *The Book of the Dead*, Ptolemaic Period.
Linen, 11.3 x 50.4 cms.
Pelizaeus-Museum, Hildesheim, LH 8

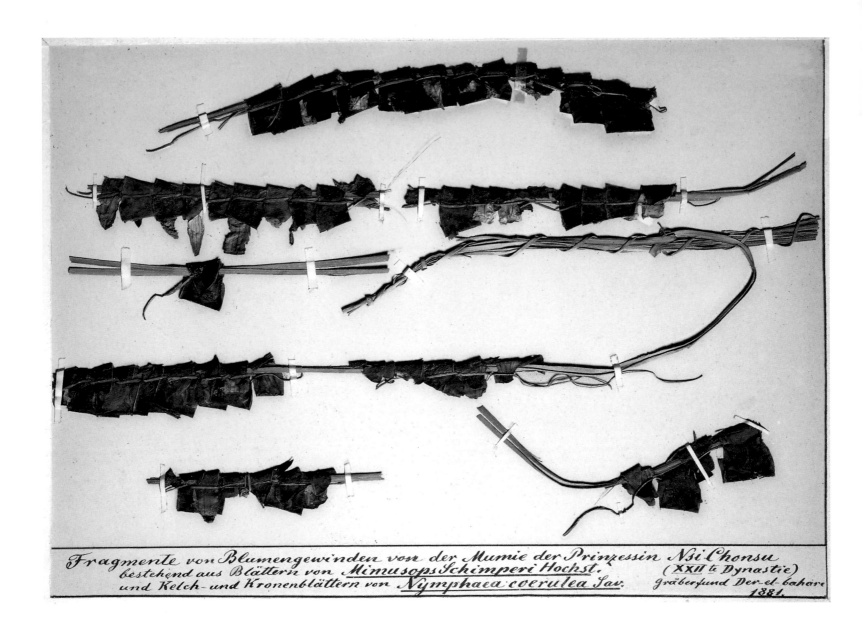

Fragmente von Blumengewinden von der Mumie der Prinzessin Nsi Chonsu (XXII te Dynastie) bestehend aus Blättern von Mimusops Schimperi Hochst. und Kelch- und Kronenblättern von Nymphaea coerulea Sav. Gräberfund Der-el-bahari 1881.

Animal amulets, of which the scarab was most widely used, were amongst the most numerous. This group also included the *ba*-bird, which represented the soul in the form of a perching falcon or one with its wings outspread, in which case it was generally made of gold (see illus. 18).

Another particularly favoured group of amulets were the small god-figures reflecting the rich variety of Egyptian gods (see illus. 19). As well as this there were the emblems of the gods: the symbols of eternity known as the *djed* pillars of Osiris, the god of the underworld, and the *tyet* girdle of his wife-sister, Isis. Other popular amulet forms represent parts of the human body, above all the *wadjet* eye and the heart.

A similar magical protective role was ascribed to strips of linen with written texts from *The Book of the Dead*. These were wound round the body of the mummy — a custom that prevailed particularly during the Ptolemaic Period. The mummy wrapping with text seen in illustration 20 is the central section of what originally was a much longer linen strip. The drawings that have survived illustrate the particularly important

seventeenth chapter of *The Book of the Dead*, containing the answers that the deceased had to be able to give to questions about the world of the gods. So the drawings show different deities, to be viewed from right to left. The two lions, flanking a horizon with a sun-disc, are 'yesterday' and 'today'. Next come the *benu*-bird and Osiris lying on a bier. The kneeling figures represent 'millions of years' and the 'great, green ocean'. Beyond two gates to the underworld, there is a drawing of the cow-goddess Mehetweret as well as the four gods 'in the retinue of Horus': Imseti, Hapy, Duamutef, and Qebehsenuef shown as canopic jars next to Osiris, who rises out of a coffin.

After the mummy had been provided with magical protection through numerous amulets and texts from *The Book of the Dead*, the embalmers would then wrap it in further layers of linen, which in turn were secured by narrow linen bands. From the 21st Dynasty onwards, the final layer of wrapping for the finest mummies was an intricately worked net of beads, as on the mummy of Tadithorpara (see illus. 73). Nets of this kind were usually made with a winged scarab and the four sons of Horus over the chest area in order to protect the viscera. On particularly elaborate mummies, these would be surrounded by yet more divine figures and symbols (see illus. 21).

Last of all, fresh leaves and flowers would be laid over the net of beads. The Egyptian floral artists who made these decorations used to entwine them on long palm fronds and link the individual garlands so that they formed rows covering the entire body of the mummy. The purpose of this floral decoration was to show that the deceased had successfully answered all the questions put by the tribunal at the Judgement of the Dead.

Some of these decorations have been preserved thanks to the Egyptian climate. Around 1000 B.C., in order to protect the mummies of earlier pharaohs from grave-robbers, the high priests of Amun of Thebes took the royal mummies from their individual tombs and reburied them together in two different caches. At this second burial, they renewed the floral decorations, which have survived to this day — a period of almost three thousand years — although the flowers have, of course, lost much of their original colour. For example, the mummy of Princess Neskhonsu (see illus. 22), reburied in the cache at Deir el-Bahri, was found with garlands of flowers made of the once darkgreen, gleaming leaves of the mimusops tree and the tender, light blue blossoms of the blue lotus, which symbolised regeneration to the Egyptians. How we should picture a full, royal floral decoration can be seen from the drawing by Georg Schweinfurth, the botanist and Africa explorer, who classified and prepared these treasures after their discovery in 1881.

When a mummy had been provided with amulets and decorated with flowers, the relatives would come and collect it from the embalmer's workshop, for then it was ready to embark on its journey into the afterlife.

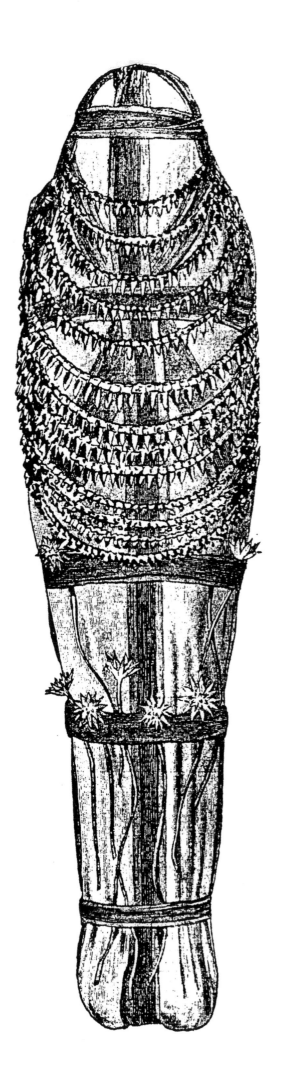

Opposite page

22   Decorations from the mummy of Neskhonsu,

Third Intermediate Period, 21st Dynasty.

Mimusops leaves and blue lotus petals, height: 24.3 cms, width: 33.5 cms.

From the royal cache at Deir el-Bahri.

Rijksmuseum van Oudheden, Leiden, Inv. AM 8

23   A royal mummy with floral decorations.

Drawing by Georg Schweinfurth, 1884

IN ANCIENT EGYPT, PEOPLE BELIEVED THAT HUMAN existence did not come to an end with death; it simply took on a different form, called the 'afterlife'. The journey from this world into the next was made by means of funerary rituals and customs. The Egyptians saw the afterlife largely as a mirror image of life as they knew it, with the same social and religious distinctions between royalty and the rest of the population. In earliest times, the belief was that kings would join the gods in heaven while non-royals would enter a realm beneath the earth, but the differences between the two were soon blurred, linking the afterlife of the kings with the realm beneath the earth and allowing the non-royal dead into heaven.

The marked difference between these two forms of afterlife as they were understood in earliest times was that after death, a king would ascend into heaven and, having joined the sun-god Ra as a member of the crew of his barque, would play a part in the daily journey of the sun. After the sun-god had gone down each evening on the western horizon, the ancient Egyptians believed that it journeyed through the underworld from west to east before appearing, rejuvenated, in the eastern sky the next morning. Travelling in the sun-barque, the king had been accepted into the world of the gods.

The afterlife of non-royal subjects, on the other hand, was imagined as an underworld situated in the necropolis — the city of the dead — and called the 'Beautiful West' in the writings of the Old Kingdom. The gate to the afterlife of the non-royal dead was a tomb in the necropolis, with the burial chamber as the threshold. By means of grave offerings and wall-paintings, the non-royal dead also took with them their life on earth into the life in the world beyond.   H.A.

IN PHARAONIC EGYPT, THE TRANSITION FROM THIS LIFE to the next was dependent on certain funeral rituals. Notions of the afterlife were expressed in the texts of spells that were to be recited during the burial ceremony. Texts relating to the king's transfiguration in heaven have been found in the 'Pyramid Texts' of the Old Kingdom. The same texts for the non-royal dead are found along with 'Coffin Texts', but not in any great numbers until the Middle Kingdom.

The individual moments of the funeral ceremony all followed a fixed 'sequence of events' and were sanctified by their sacramental significance. Each individual moment in the ritual related to an event in the world of the gods. In royal funerals, major importance was attached to the basic concept of the sun-god crossing the nightly firmament, while in non-royal funerals equal importance was attached to the Osiris myth, which was particularly relevant to the funeral ceremony in that it tells of the god's death and resurrection. Parallels can readily be drawn between the fate of the individual in death and that of the god Osiris as he died and came to life again. In addition to this, the realm of the god Osiris was believed to be located in the underworld, another close link with the afterlife of the non-royal dead.

Depictions of the various phases of ritual burials have been found in the tombs of officials dating from the Old, Middle, and New Kingdoms, with yet more illustrations in the New Kingdom version of the *Book of the Dead* (one of several). Furthermore, there is a written account of ancient Egyptian burial practices in a literary work from the Middle Kingdom which tells of Sinuhe, who fled in the early days of the 12th Dynasty to Palestine, but later returned to Egypt. The turning point of 'The Story of Sinuhe' is a letter from the pharaoh to Sinuhe, now an

25   Incense burner, Third Intermediate Period, 22nd–25th Dynasty.

Bronze, length: 60.5 cms.

From the Temple of Amun at El-Hibe.

Ägyptologisches Institut der Universität Heidelberg, Inv. 2419

26   *Hes* vase (solid). Middle Kingdom.

Faience, height: 17.3 cms.

Pelizaeus–Museum, Hildesheim, Inv. 1640.

Vessel to hold purifying water for the deceased in the afterlife

24   Funerary ritual from the burial papyrus of Hunefer,

New Kingdom, 19th Dynasty

old man, in Palestine. In it, the pharaoh tries to persuade him to return home with the promise of a ritual burial in Egypt, contrasting Egyptian customs with the barbaric practice of bundling the body into a goatskin and burying it under a pile of stones. The king promises how it would be in Egypt:

> ... *at night you would be anointed with pine oil and bound in*
> *wrappings made by Tait, the goddess of weaving.*
> *A procession will take place on the day of your burial.*
> *The inner coffin will be made of gold, its head will be of*
> *lapis lazuli.*
> *Heaven is above you as you lie on the bier.*
> *Oxen will draw you, a chorus of singers will precede you.*
> *At the entrance to your tomb the dance of the 'Weary'*
> *(that is, the Dead) will be performed.*
> *The list of offerings will be recited for you.*
> *There will be a slaughter at the entrance to your tomb.*
> *The pillars (of your burial chamber) are made of white limestone ...*

The description of the funeral ceremony given by the king in his letter to Sinuhe matches exactly the depictions known to us from the New Kingdom. These show how oxen would draw the mummy, lying on a bier placed on a carriage, to the necropolis. In the papyrus of Hunefer (see illus. 24), a mummy is seen in a ritual barque with the deceased's sarcophagus under a baldachin. A priest wearing a panther's skin accompanies the mummy. Incense dispersed by the priest prepares the way, while water poured from a *hes* vase symbolises purification (cf. illus. 26). The participants in such processions were the relatives of the deceased and his or her friends, neighbours, and colleagues. The main procession would be followed by a small sled with the canopic jars under the protection of Anubis, the jackal-headed god of the dead.

THE OPENING OF THE MOUTH

THE BELIEF THAT DEATH WAS NOT THE END OF LIFE BUT the transition into an afterlife underpinned both mummification and the elaborate rituals of the funeral ceremony. The deceased could only take up a place in the afterlife if his or her body was intact and provided with the necessary grave goods. Closely linked to the notion of an individual's continued existence in a world reflecting our own was the question of how the deceased was to be provided with food and other necessary items after burial. Clearly, plans had to be made for this. After the Old Kingdom, a special ritual was developed to restore the senses and soul of the deceased. The Egyptians themselves called this ritual the 'Opening of the Mouth' (*upet-ra*).

27   Fishtail knife, Prehistoric Period or Early Dynastic Period.

Flint, length: 20 cms.

Pelizaeus-Museum, Hildesheim, Inv. 5106

Opposite page

28   Set for the ceremony of the Opening of the Mouth, Old Kingdom.

Plaster alabaster, limestone, argillite, chlorite slate, ivory, flint, plaster,

17.5 x 11.5 cms.

Ägyptisches Museum der Universität Leipzig, Inv. 5330

The ceremony of the Opening of the Mouth was originally intended for the ritual giving of life to tomb statues. When the ceremony later came to be performed on mummies, the same utensils used for the statues were employed again. This explains why most of these tools are the same as those used by early sculptors, who usually worked in ivory or wood. The adze used for the opening of the mouth, eyes, ears, and nose came from the carpenter's workshop and is still a widely used woodworking tool.

Another tool, an old-fashioned one, used in the Opening of the Mouth ceremony was the 'fish-tail knife' with a frontal blade in the form of a fish tail (see illus. 27). These knives, which go back to the Stone Age, continued even in later times to be made of flint, presumably due to the belief that this stone possessed magical properties. The touch of the knife's blade magically 'opened' the lips far enough for the statue — or the mummy — to take food and drink offered to it.

From the Old Kingdom onwards, the traditional utensils for this ceremony were assembled as small sets for the deceased's use and then included as part of the grave goods (see illus. 28). The tools in question were not necessarily precisely those that would have been used in this life and often turn out to be rather undersized. In fact, these sets of mouth-opening tools are only imitations of real tools and would never have been usable in actuality. Although they are more like model tools, for the priest they were no less effective and all he needed to ensure the Opening of the Mouth.

Like the burial ceremony, the Opening of the Mouth ceremony was depicted on walls of chapels in the tombs of high officials from the New Kingdom onwards. From there, they found their way into illustrations in *The Book of the Dead,* where the ceremony of the Opening of the Mouth in front of the tomb is shown as the final stage of the burial procession.

A detailed representation of the Opening of the Mouth before the tomb is contained in Hunefer's *Book of the Dead* from the beginning of the 19th Dynasty (see illus. 29). At the right-hand edge of the picture, there is a tomb below a pyramid; in the left foreground in front of the tomb is a tomb stela with the text of the offering prayer. At the entrance to the tomb is an upright mummy, supported by a priest who wears an Anubis mask and has one arm round the body of the mummy. At the mummy's feet, a female mourner kneels, while a second mourner stands facing it. Both raise their right hands in gestures of grief, strewing ashes on their heads. Behind the women, the cult's officiators can be seen engaged in the ceremony of the Opening of the Mouth. In the front row, there are two priests, although their arms and hands seem to suggest the presence of three people because they are performing three rituals. One hand holds a wooden adze, two hands hold four round jars which are being used in a cleansing process, and a further hand in the background grasps a snake-stick, which is being lifted towards the mouth of the mummy for the Opening of the Mouth.

Behind these priests stands the most important priest in the scene, the *sem* priest, dressed in a panther's skin. In his left hand, he delicately holds an incense burner, and in his right he has a libation vase with a spout for purification rituals. The spell to be recited during the ceremony is shown in vertical rows above the scene. On a mat in front of the *sem* priest lie the offerings of food, which include a large number of round unleavened loaves.

The Opening of the Mouth was performed not only on the mummy but also on the mummiform coffin containing the deceased. This explains why, in many tombs dating from the New Kingdom which have depictions of this ceremony, it seems that there are two mummies in front of the tomb. In fact, only one of these is the actual mummy, while the other is a coffin shaped to contain it.   H. A.

29   The ceremony of the Opening of the Mouth from the burial papyrus of Hunefer, New Kingdom, 19th Dynasty

MUMMIFORM COFFINS

THE EARLIEST MUMMIFORM COFFINS DATE FROM THE Middle Kingdom. In the 21st and early 22nd Dynasties, the iconography of coffins was at its most developed. One reason for this was the increase in grave robbery and the consequent desecration of mummies by grave robbers. The once lavishly decorated individual private tombs with their grave goods were now abandoned in favour of multiple tombs in secret caches. This development resulted in elements of the decorative paintings on tomb walls being transferred to the coffins, where the limited space available meant that only the most important texts and scenes from the tomb decorations could be accommodated — for example, the offering prayer and offering rites.

A fine example of decoration on a mummy case is found on the cartonnage case made for Pabasa in the Third Intermediate Period (see illus. 30). It is made of painted, moulded linen and plaster and forms a cover for the mummified body. The arms are integral with the body, and below the wig the hands are disproportionately small. Between the hands, there is an amulet with a painted scarab in the centre.

The upper part of the case shows the head framed by a wig in three sections, while the mummy's upper body is obscured by a floral collar. The face is delicately modelled. The wig reaches to the chest, where it is finished with floral decorations. It is hidden above the forehead by the hood of a vulture with a back-curving body. The bird's finely detailed wings frame the face, touching the strands of the wig.

The lower part of the case has illustrations depicting scenes from the wrapping of the mummy. These start just below the collar with a representation of the underworld sun-god with his ram's head and out-spread falcon's wings. A narrow vertical strip in the centre contains the sacrificial prayer to the god of the dead, Ptah-Sokar-Osiris, and gives the name of the deceased. On either side of this, there are five sections with religious scenes in a symmetrical arrangement. The top section shows the guardian gods — Imseti and Qebehsenuef on the left, with Hapy and Duamutef on the right — each linked to a scene from the embalming rituals. In the register below this, the deceased is shown worshipping the sun-god Horakhty. The third section depicts the judgement of the deceased with one of the forty-two judges and the monster known as 'the Gobbler'. For if the deceased was found guilty of misdemeanours, this monster would devour his or her heart — i.e., his or her soul. The fourth section shows the deceased worshipping the cow-goddess Mehetweret, who rose from the primeval floods when the earth was created and became one of the first living creatures in our world. At the lowest level, protective Osiris, Isis, and Nephthys can be seen as winged, guardian snake-deities.

The ground colour of the case is dark green. The drawings and the texts are in yellow, with traces of an inner drawing in red and green. The vulture's hood over the wig and the floral finishings at the bottom of the wig indicate that the original occupant of the cartonnage case was a woman, which is further confirmed by the yellow colour of the face. Everything points to the case, once made for a woman, having been reworked to contain the body of a man.

Various features of this case place it in the Third Intermediate Period, most probably during the reign of Osorkon I (around 900 B.C.). It was found in a wooden mummiform coffin painted a reddish brown. The decoration on the outer coffin is sparing and shows only the face of the deceased and the long wig, lying in three sections. The ends of the wig, like that on the cartonnage case, are finished with floral decorations. Lastly, a vertical strip with black hieroglyphs contains the offering prayer to the gods of the dead.

H.A.

30   Cartonnage case of Pabasa, Third Intermediate Period, c. 900 B.C.

Plaster soaked linen, length: 180 cms.

Museum für Völkerkunde, Hamburg, Inv. 4057b

EMBALMING AND THE STRICT OBSERVANCE OF BURIAL rituals with the restoration of the senses in the Opening of the Mouth ceremony ensured that the deceased would be able to enter the next world. But the deceased could not exist in the afterlife without a soul. Therefore, the way for the soul to make the same journey also had to be prepared. This was the reason for the scrutiny of the heart at the Judgement of the Dead.

Notions of a tribunal after death, where a person's deeds were believed to be judged as good or bad, went back to the days of the Old Kingdom. In the non-royal tomb inscriptions from those days, there are already references to a court in the afterlife, much like one on earth. Its members would gather when a complainant came forward to make an accusation, and only those who had led good and blameless lives would escape trial. The best way to achieve this was by 'being just and truthful' during one's days on earth, by making no enemies and living according to the ethics of the day. Idealised biographies in tomb inscriptions record lives in formulaic terms:

> I gave bread to the hungry and clothes to the naked.
> I carried the traveller in my boat …
> I never spoke ill of anyone or of any ruler because I wanted
> the Great God to view me with favour.
> I never judged in any dispute in such a way that a son was robbed
> of his father's inheritance.

During the New Kingdom, the judgements and the form of the tribunal underwent one major change. Now, it was not a matter of the deceased being examined in response to a particular case or accusation — now, everyone had to go before the tribunal, whose members then judged the whole of that person's life. And the highest judge was omniscient, for he was Osiris, the god of the underworld. Only those who made it past the judges would be able to continue their existence in the afterlife.

The very routine nature of this tribunal became a weakness in that, in order to pass, it was enough simply to state that one had 'not committed' certain potential misdeeds. From these statements, we can gain a picture of the moral code which governed human life and the relationship of the individual to the gods and to his or her fellow human beings. These so-called 'negative confessions' appeared in classic form during the New Kingdom in *The Book of the Dead* (chap. 125) and took in numerous possible human misdemeanours, as in these examples:

> I have not despised God. I have not caused misery; nor have I
> worked affliction. I have done not that which God doth abominate.
> I have caused no wrong to be done to the servant by his master.
> I have not committed murder; nor have I ever bidden any man

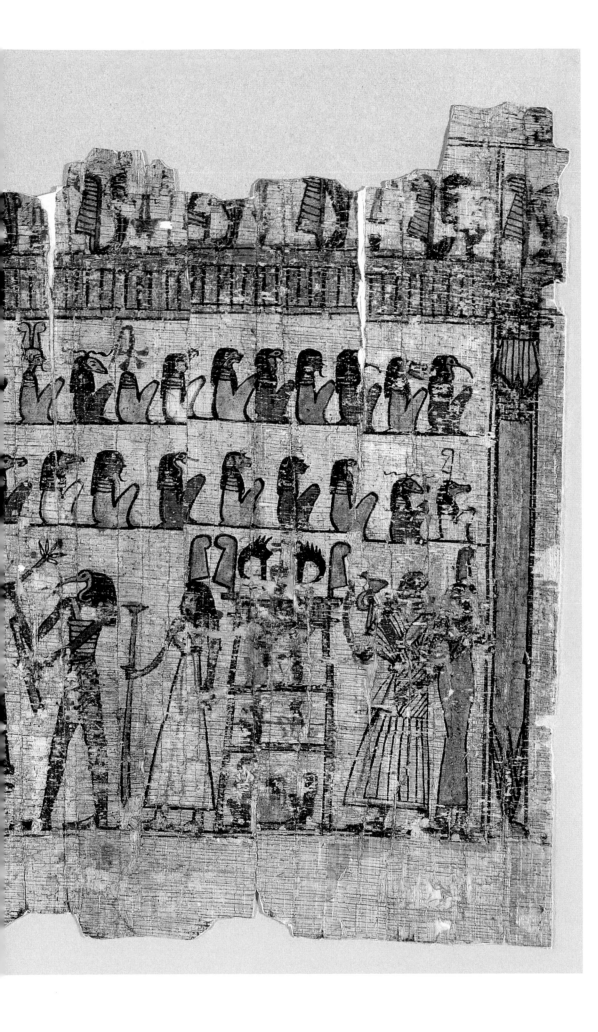

31 Burial papyrus of Nesnakht (excerpt),
c. 300 B.C.
Dimension of detail: 34 x 55 cms.
Rijksmuseum van Oudheden, Leiden,
Inv. Cl 11a Bl. 4

to slay on my behalf. I have not wronged the people.
I have not added to the weight of the balance; nor have I made light
the weight in the scales.
I have not snatched the milk from the mouth of the babe. I have not
driven the cattle from their pastures.
I have not snared the water-fowl of the gods. I have not caught
fishes with bait of their own bodies.

The judgement process is depicted in the exhaustive New Kingdom *Book of the Dead*, which shows the weighing of the heart in front of Osiris and forty-two assessor-gods. While the deceased, claiming innocence, makes 'negative confessions', the heart is placed on one side of a set of scales and weighed against a figurine of the goddess of truth. If the heart is caught making a false statement and found to be burdened by sin, the scale will sink and the heart will be devoured by 'the Gobbler'. Further measures are undertaken to avoid being condemned by the assessor gods. Spell 30B of *The Book of the Dead* impresses upon the heart, as it lies on the scales, that it should not speak out against the deceased during the judgement. The mummy is also provided with a heart scarab with this spell inscribed on its base.

Following a favourable judgement by the tribunal, the 'justified' deceased is taken up into Osiris's kingdom. The soul rejoins the body, and their existence continues in the afterlife. The free-flying soul-bird can leave the tomb as it wishes, rise up into the daylight, and return again to the mummy. The notion of the temporary separation and coming together in the afterlife is embodied in the New Kingdom by the small figure of Ipy (cf. illus. 32), shown holding his *ba* against his body while in his other hand grasping a *djed* pillar.

The idea of the justified deceased, whose senses and soul have been restored, continuing to exist in the realm of Osiris is found on a 19th-Dynasty tombstone in the necropolis at Per-Ramesse in the East Delta region (see illus. 33). The 'justified' stela owner, Nebamun, approaches Osiris and, with a worshipful gesture, offers him a spray of flowers. Osiris is shown as a mummy seated on his throne, holding a sceptre and scourge in his hands, the insignia of his power in the afterlife. The topmost roundel of the stela is crowned with a pyramid showing the god Anubis, the Keeper of the Balance at the weighing of the heart. The deceased is not depicted as a mummy, but as a living person with a long, straight wig, dressed for his role as an official.   H.A.

GRAVE GOODS FOR THE AFTERLIFE

THE EGYPTIANS WERE VERY CONCERNED THAT THEY might be called on to do physical work in the afterlife for Osiris. In order to avoid this, they turned to magical means which had been tested for generations and which had proved to be effective 'a million times'. The relevant texts have been found in Middle Kingdom Coffin Texts and in the New Kingdom *Book of the Dead*. The most potent help was apparently to be had from *shabti*s. These are figures inscribed with the name of the deceased which became active whenever their owner was called out by name to work. They answered instead of the deceased (*shabti* means 'answerer') and carried out the required work in place of the deceased.

Most *shabti*s are shaped like mummies. They carry hoes on their shoulders and sacks on their backs for the work they will be doing in the fields. The ideal would be for the deceased to have three hundred and sixty of these figures, one for each day of the year, allowing for five work-free days. These figures are supervised by thirty-six overseers, working on the basis of ten-day weeks. The overseers are generally without tools. *Shabti*s are often inscribed with a text that is found in full in Chapter 6 of *The Book of the Dead*:

> 'Hail, shabti figure! If it be decreed that Osiris shall do any of the
> work which is to be done in the underworld, let all that standeth in
> the way be removed from before him; whether it be to plough the
> fields, or to fill the channels with water or to carry the sand from
> the East to the West.' The shabti figure replies: 'I will do it; verily
> I am here when thou callest.'

It is interesting that kings also have such *shabti*s to carry out any work to be done in the afterworld. In Tutanchamun's tomb, several series depicting such workers were found.   H.A.

Opposite page

35   Four *shabti*s, Late Period.

Faience, height: 12.3 cms, 26 cms, 9.3 cms, 18.3 cms.

Museum für Kunst und Gewerbe, Hamburg,

Inv. 1919.165, 1953.81, 1919.164, 1917.92

34   *Shabti* figure Queen Henut-tani, rear view

with small sand-bag,

Third Intermediate Period, 21st Dynasty.

Faience, height: 11.8 cms.

Deir-el-Bahari.

Pelizaeus-Museum, Hildesheim

THE DECEASED AND OSIRIS

IT WAS THE FATE OF THE GOD OSIRIS THAT ALLOWED THE deceased to hope for regeneration and reanimation in the realm of the dead.

First references to Osiris date back to the Old Kingdom, since which time he had been revered as the king and ruler of the underworld. In his role as the king of the dead, he complemented his son Horus, who sat on the throne of the living. Osiris was the dead ruler, Horus the living king. After his death, Osiris was mourned, mummified, buried, and provided for. The rituals of mummification and the restoration of his senses and his soul led to his resurrection in the afterlife. As a king-god, he wears a white crown and holds a sceptre and scourge.

Although Osiris, as a god, was bound up with human existence, his rebirth is symbolised by an image from the plant world and compared to a growing seed. During the New Kingdom, this connection led to the notion of 'Cornosiris', represented as a negative relief of a recumbent Osiris figure hollowed out of a clay brick (see illus. 37). This figure was filled with earth and corn seeds. The seeds were watered and sprouted, demonstrating the strength of the resurrected Osiris working through the soil.

The resurrection of Osiris is also expressed in the composite figure of Ptah-Sokar-Osiris (see illus. 38). These figures, very common in the Late Period, depict the resurrected Osiris in syncretic form as the Memphitic god of the dead. He is identified with the particular deceased person whose name is given in a vertical band. These mummiform figures, wearing a crown with a double feather and ram's horns, stand on a small casket, with a lid decorated with a statuette of a mummified falcon. The casket itself contains a Cornosiris. The combination of a recumbent falcon and a Cornosiris shows this to be the grave of Osiris. At the same time, the standing figure of Ptah-Sokar-Osiris represents the resurrection of Osiris from out of the Cornosiris. Since the figure of Ptah-Sokar-Osiris is identified with a particular deceased person, the resurrection also applies to that individual. The function of these figures is to make clear the link between the fate of the deceased and that of Osiris.

The interpretation of the casket as the grave of Osiris lends these figures a significance greater even than death itself. They show the resurrected god Ptah-Sokar-Osiris on the grave of Osiris, which at the same time symbolises the original mound which generated all creation and which will restore order to the world. In this figure, there is a powerful union of death and resurrection, albeit with the paradox that the deceased is set on a par both with the dead god and the god that comes back to life. Statuettes of this kind symbolise death and resurrection at one and the same time, thereby linking the two opposed conditions of humans in the afterlife.   H.A.

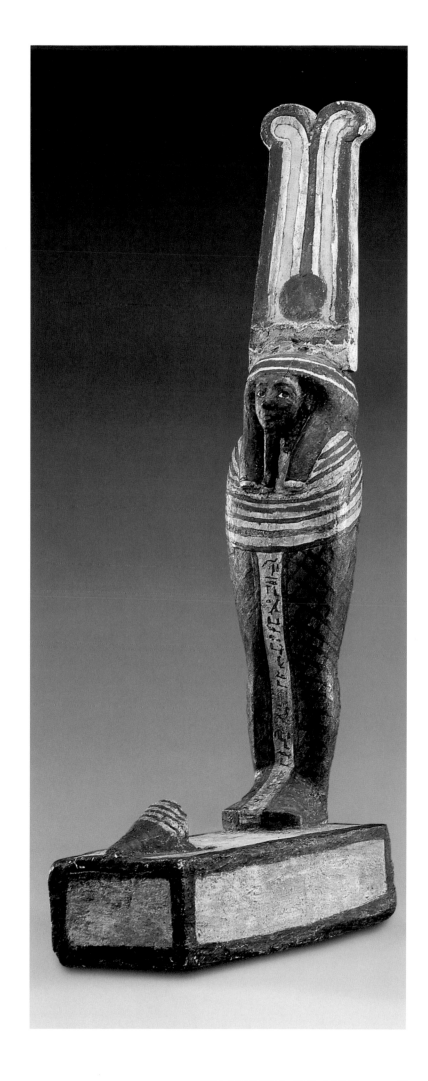

Opposite page

36   Osiris, Late Period, c. 600 B.C.

Bronze, height: 75 cms.

Museum für Kunst und Gewerbe, Hamburg,

Inv. 1956.129/St. 12

37   Corn Osiris, Late Period, 6th-5th century B.C.

Clay, height: 6 cms.

Pelizaeus-Museum, Hildesheim, Inv. 4550

38   Ptah-Sokar-Osiris, Ptolemaic.

Painted wood, height: 54 cms.

Pelizaeus-Museum, Hildesheim, Inv. LH 2

CLUES FROM CANOPIC JARS

WE HAVE A GREAT DEAL OF INFORMATION ABOUT THE religious beliefs that led to mummification in pharaonic Egypt. But we do not know exactly when the Egyptians first attempted to preserve the bodies of their dead from decay by embalming them. At first — probably at the beginning of the third millennium B.C. — the arms, legs, and body were securely wrapped in strips of linen. Later, a face would be painted on the linen, and individual body parts like breasts and genitalia would be modelled out of material. Then linen was laid over these as clothing. The deceased was made to appear as true to life as possible.

The Egyptians recognised early on that bodily decay started in the viscera of the chest and abdominal cavities, so they took the decisive step of making an incision into the abdominal cavity and removing the organs. So that the deceased should remain whole, the organs were not disposed of, but wrapped individually in linen and buried in the tomb. In the earliest days, the packages of organs were probably laid in a particular area in the tomb, only being placed in special canopic jars somewhat later. There were always four jars, one for each organ.

The designation *canopic* goes back to the scholar Athanasius Kircher (1602–80), who made an intensive study of the culture of ancient Egypt. He mistakenly took the jar-shaped figure of Osiris as a representation of Canopus, the pilot of Menelaus, and this idea was transferred to the jars used to hold organs. The oldest records of canopic jars come from the graves of Queen Hetepheres, the mother of Cheops, and of his grand-daughter Meriesankh. Such jars are not found in the tombs of private individuals until later, and then as plain *nemset* vases with a flat lid worked in chalkstone, alabaster, or fired clay. In fact, it is wrong to think that after the Old Kingdom, the viscera were always removed from the body and carefully packed. At this distance in time, it is barely possible to tell *what* had been removed from the very badly preserved mummies from the Old Kingdom, and as late as the Middle Kingdom, pieces of the internal organs were often left inside the body. Even when the chest and abdominal cavities were empty, the organs were not necessarily to be found in canopic jars, for some had little space inside them or were in fact fake jars and not hollow at all (see illus. 40). According to prevalent religious beliefs, it was enough to place the jars in the tomb along with the body to provide it with magical protection. Thus far, no remains of organs have been found in the canopic jars from private individuals' tombs dating from the Old Kingdom, and it was only in the canopic caskets belonging to Queen Hetepheres that wrapped organs were found in a natron solution.

It was during the early years of the Middle Kingdom that the first canopic jars with human heads emerged; indeed, the whole vessel might be made in human form with little arms and legs. These canopic jars generally, although not always, contained packages of organs, the body cavities having meanwhile been refilled with sawdust or linen. As well as anthropomorphic canopic jars, there are also plain alabaster vessels, predominantly in the royal necropolis in Dahshur. These are either narrow ovals with a flat lid or jar-shaped with a convex lid surmounted by a pommel (cf. illus. 41 and 42).

39   Canopic jars and *shabti* figures being made.

Theban tomb painting from the New Kingdom.

40 Canopic jars and pseudo
canopic jars, Old Kingdom,
5th and 6th Dynasty.
Limestone, height: 30 cms
and 34 cms.
From Giza.
Pelizaeus-Museum,
Hildesheim,
Inv. 3106 and 3251

41 Canopic jar,
Middle Kingdom.
Alabaster, height: 33 cms.
From Dashur.
Rijksmuseum van Oudheden,
Leiden, Inv. AAL 9b

42 Canopic jar,
Middle Kingdom.
Alabaster, height: 32 cms.
From Dashur.
Rijksmuseum van Oudheden,
Leiden, Inv. AAL 3c

43   Canopic jar belonging to Hui with an invocation to the goddess

Isis and to Imseti, one of the sons of Horus, 18th Dynasty.

Terracotta, height: 38 cms.

Rijksmuseum van Oudheden, Leiden, Inv. Cl 258

44   Canopic jars belonging to Tanetdjedkhy, late New Kingdom.

Limestone, height: c. 30 cms.

Pelizaeus-Museum, Hildesheim, Inv. LH 18

From the Middle Kingdom onwards, the organs in canopic jars were placed under the protection of four deities, the sons of Horus, Imseti, Hapy, Duamutef, and Qebehsenuef. An invocation in the form of a lengthy inscription, including the name of the deceased, on the front of the jar was customarily addressed to the four sons together with the goddesses Isis, Nephthys, Selket, and Neith.

In the early days of the New Kingdom, canopic lids took the form of human heads. Later, in the 19th Dynasty, we find instead the heads of the four sons of Horus: Imseti, the guardian of the liver, as a human being; Hapy, responsible for the lungs, as an ape; Qebehsenuef as a falcon, to watch over the intestines; and Duamutef as a jackal, to protect the stomach.

Typical of this period are the canopic jars from the tomb of Tanetdjedkhy, 'the daughter of Djedkhy' (see illus. 44). Intriguingly, the inscription on the jar with the ape-headed stopper has an error in it, for it is not Hapy that is being addressed here, but Imseti, who has already been correctly named on the second jar with the human-headed lid. This error suggests that jars and lids were produced separately for use as they were needed. For the burial of Tanetdjedkhy, the embalmers mistakenly selected two identical jars with the invocation to the god Imseti, but used the lids with the heads of Hapy and Imseti.

Brains were also occasionally removed from the skull as early as the Middle Kingdom, a practice that became the rule amongst embalmers during the course of the New Kingdom. Brains were not preserved in canopic jars.

In the 21st Dynasty, a completely new way of handling the viscera emerged suddenly. Now, the embalmers laid the organs, or parts of them, out on a linen cloth, placed a wax figure of the relevant guardian god on the organs (cf. illus. 45), and then rolled everything together as one package. After the mummification of the body, they would insert the packages of organs through the opening in the abdomen wall into the chest and abdominal cavities. During the 25th Dynasty, it again became fashionable to pack the organs in canopic jars, but organs were often still rolled up and returned to the body right up to the Ptolemaic Period, albeit now without wax figures of the sons of Horus. From the 26th until the 30th Dynasty — that is, until Egypt was conquered by Alexander the Great — canopic jars made of alabaster were particularly popular. The organs contained in these were often immersed in resinous embalming oils that filled the jar right up to the top. Large amounts of these same oils were now also used for embalming bodies.

After this time, other kinds of canopic containers occasionally were used, such as ceramic or wooden caskets in which all four organs were placed together. Ceramic containers as in illustration 46 are extremely

45   Duamutef, one of the sons of Horus,
Third Intermediate Period, 21st Dynasty.
Wax, height: 9.5 cms.
Rijksmuseum van Oudheden, Leiden, Inv. AC 5

46   Container for viscera,
Late Period to Ptolemaic Period.
Painted terracotta, height: 28 cms.
Pelizaeus-Museum, Hildesheim, Inv. 1644

Opposite page
47   Casket for viscera. 30th Dynasty
to Ptolemaic Period.
Wood, height: 67 cms.
From Deir el-Bahri.
Rijksmuseum van Oudheden, Leiden,
Inv. AH 215

rare. The painted decorations show three of the four sons of Horus, seated on this occasion, and a scene in which a woman makes an offering to the mummified god Osiris, crouched on the floor.

Slightly more common were wooden canopic caskets like that of Hornedjitef. This man bore the title of Father of God and Prophet of Amun in Karnak. His mummy is now in the British Museum, London (EA 6679), while his canopic casket is in the Rijksmuseum van Oudheden, Leiden (see illus. 47). The casket is in the form of an ancient Egyptian shrine. On the lid, there is a wooden figure in the form of a falcon mummy, representing the god Sokar, who was thought to assist the deceased in their resurrection after death. The decorations on the sides of the casket show the four sons of Horus, and the front has two depictions of Anubis before a shrine to Osiris with strips of linen and incense burners in his hands.

The practice of placing canopic jars containing the removed viscera into the tomb with the mummy did not die out in Egypt until the Roman period.

ANIMAL MUMMIES

Some of the Egyptians hold crocodiles sacred … after death the crocodiles are embalmed and buried in sacred coffins.

HERODOTUS II.69

GREEK AND ROMAN TRAVELLERS FOUND TO THEIR GREAT astonishment that the Egyptian populace revered sacred animals. These were kept in temples, given special food, and sometimes even bedecked with jewellery, and when they died they were given elaborate funerals. In the same vein, temple statues of gods and depictions of them in reliefs and tomb paintings occurred in the shapes of animals or in combined human and animal forms.

This form of divine worship was very much part of the Egyptian way of life. The Egyptians believed that a deity could manifest itself in a living animal. Such creatures would then be seen as the 'god's *ba*', which can be understood as the 'god's power'. Particularly important were, for example, the sacred Apis bulls at Memphis, believed to embody the god Ptah. The burial place of these bulls, the so-called Serapeum at Saqqara, consisted of extended underground galleries with huge stone sarcophagi which once contained the embalmed bodies of the bulls. In the ruins of the Temple of Ptah at Memphis, it is still possible to see the alabaster tables used for embalming the Apis bulls.

After the Late Period, and particularly during the Graeco-Roman period, there was an increase in animal cults in Egypt. Now, it was not simply individual animals that were seen as gods in animal form; all animals were held to be sacred. Different animals were revered according to region, and their underground burial places were attached to temples. Towards the end of the time of the pharaohs, there was an increase in animal cults particularly amongst the ordinary people. By offering either a small bronze figure of a sacred animal or an elaborately packed mummy, an individual could make direct contact with the deity.

Opposite page

48   Stela of the head goldsmith Panweret, inscribed with an offering prayer to the crocodile-shaped god Sobek, New Kingdom, 19th Dynasty.
Limestone, height: 23 cms.
From Qantir.
Pelizaeus-Museum, Hildesheim, Inv. 398

49   Cat's head with an earring, Late Period, c. 7th-6th century B.C.
Bronze and gold, height: 10 cms.
Museum für Kunst und Gewerbe, Hamburg, Inv. 1924.168

The list of animals in which gods were believed to manifest themselves is lengthy and still growing as animal cemeteries are excavated and more mummies are examined.

THE CROCODILE

As early as the third millennium B.C., the crocodile was regarded as sacred, and it remained so until the Roman era. It was seen above all as the embodiment of the god Sobek, and as a result there were large crocodile cemeteries in Fayum and Kom Ombo, the main cult centres of this god. But there was also a famous burial place for crocodiles in Maabdah, north of present-day Assiut. Fully grown crocodiles were buried there in coffins or cartonnage cases, while smaller animals (sixty to eighty in number) or eggs were packed in baskets.

Besides bronze figures, the Egyptians also used to set up small temple stelae for their gods in animal form. These show the person who made the dedication making an offering or praying to the deity (see illus. 48).

THE CAT

There were a number of cat-shaped deities, foremost amongst them being the goddess Bastet. The faithful offered countless bronze figures to her temples, showing her either as a cat, often with an earring (see illus. 49), as a suckling mother cat, or in the form of a cat-headed woman with a basket on her arm.

50 Cat, Late Period.

Bronze, height: 13.6 cms.

Museum für Kunst und Gewerbe, Hamburg,

Inv. 1917.1427

51 Mummified cat, Late Period to Ptolemaic Period.

Height: 51.5 cms.

Pelizaeus-Museum, Hildesheim, Inv. 1679

Cat mummies have survived in large numbers. In Beni Hasan, the cats' cemetery was so extensive that in modern times these mummies were simply dug up to be used as fertiliser.

THE IBIS

The ibis was the creature associated with Thoth, the god of truth and the gods' scribe. Mummified birds would be wrapped in linen strips, often woven into intricate patterns (see illus. 52) and offered to the god as votive gifts. The most elaborate ibis mummies would sometimes even have a gilded wooden ibis head with an *atef* crown (see illus. 53).

In some cases, bird mummies were laid in small wooden coffins, but usually they were placed in special clay jars with a lid. Even today, these are stacked in their tens of thousands in the ibis catacombs at Saqqara (see illus. 54). As long ago as the eighteenth century, these clay burial vessels or even the ibis mummies themselves were favourite souvenirs for travellers returning from Egypt.

52 Two ibis mummies,
Ptolemaic Period.
Length: 31.5 and 23 cms.
Pelizaeus-Museum,
Hildesheim, LH 9, LH 10

53 Ibis head with *atef* crown
from an ibis mummy, Ptolemaic Period.
Gold-plated wood,
length: 34.5 cms.
Pelizaeus-Museum,
Hildesheim, LH 15

54 Coffin for an ibis
mummy, Late Period –
Ptolemaic Period.
Clay, length: 37 cms.
Pelizaeus-Museum,
Hildesheim, Inv. 5466

55 Horus falcon,
Late Period,
29th-30th Dynasty.
Bronze,
height: 22.5 cms.
Museum für Kunst
und Gewerbe,
Hamburg,
Inv. 1892.34

The sun-god Ra was embodied as a falcon. These birds were also often buried in small coffins. Since the birds' tail-feathers were sometimes too long for the coffins, the embalmers simply made a bend in the feathers, thus resulting in hook-shaped mummies (see illus. 56).

THE SCARAB

The scarab beetle was also seen as an embodiment of the sun-god Ra, particularly of the morning sun. The scarab was the symbol of regeneration, of reanimation after death, and for this reason was one of the most widely used amulets. Desiccated beetles, packed into small caskets, were buried in animal cemeteries as votive gifts along with other animal mummies (see illus. 57).

Two of the more unusual animal mummies are the shrew and the snake, both manifestations of the god of creation, Atum. In some instances, these creatures were even wrapped together (see illus. 57).

56   Two falcon mummies, Ptolemaic.

Length: 37.2 cms and 36.7 cms.

Pelizaeus-Museum, Hildesheim, Inv. LH 12 and LH 13

57   Two small wooden boxes, one for a scarab, and the other containing a mummified shrew wrapped in linen and a small snake, Ptolemaic.

Length: 6 cms and 9 cms.

Pelizaeus-Museum, Hildesheim, Inv. LH 16 and LH 17

Two deities, Anubis and Wepwawet, were depicted as a dog or a jackal. It is not possible to tell which of these two closely related members of the Canidae family is being portrayed, nor was this necessarily of concern to the Egyptians. These creatures are always black in colour and have large, bushy tails. When Anubis is being represented, he is shown lying down. Wepwawet is portrayed standing up on a standard.

Anubis had two functions. One was his role as the god who watched over the embalming process, in which case he was depicted with an animal's head, bending over a mummy lying on a lion-shaped bier (see illus. 61). In his other role, Anubis was the guardian of the necropolis. In the Graeco-Roman period, he was clearly identified as a dog, so he was offered dog mummies as votive gifts. Particularly lavishly worked dog mummies would be placed in painted cartonnage cases just like those of human beings. In the example shown in illustration 58, the face is that of a dog. On the front of the cartonnage, there are colourful garlands of flowers and two seated dogs, a dark one and a lighter one, on either side of an *ankh*, the symbol of life. The back and sides are decorated with a pattern of beads. Professor Angela von den Driesch, University of Munich, has examined an X-ray of the mummy package from this cartonnage case (see illus. 59). It reveals two complete bodies of young dogs and the skeleton of a third, although the X-ray does not show the third dog's head.

In the Late Period and Ptolemaic Period, black-painted Anubis figures were often mounted on coffin lids to protect the body of the deceased (see illus. 60).

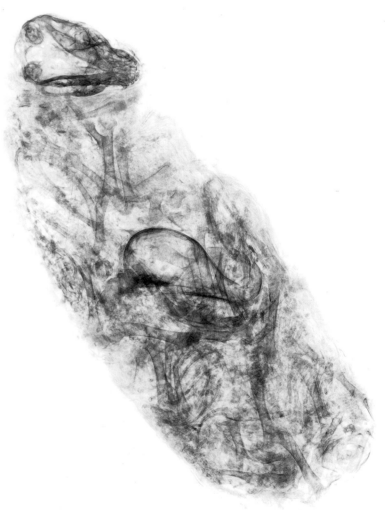

Opposite page

58   Cartonnage case for the mummified dog,
Paketes, Roman.
Height: 23 cms.
Pelizaeus-Museum, Hildesheim, Inv. LH 7

59   X-ray of the mummified dog, Paketes.
(see illus. 58)

60   The figure of Anubis from a coffin, Late Period.
Wood, height: 18.3 cms.
Museum für Kunst und Gewerbe, Hamburg,
Inv. 1996.162

61   Anubis attending a mummy lying on its bier,
outline for a wall painting, Ptolemaic Period.
From Denderah

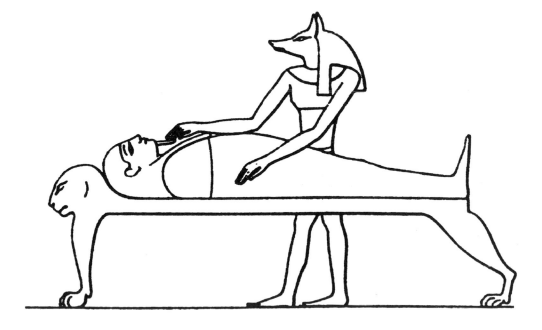

BURIALS DURING THE MIDDLE KINGDOM

An offering that the king gives and Osiris, Lord of Busiris, the great god, Lord of Abydos, an offering to the dead of bread, ale, cattle, fowl, pure linen, incense, embalming oil, and all the beautiful and pure things from which a god lives, the noble Khnumhotep.

THE INVOCATION ABOVE, MADE IN THE HOPE OF ACHIEVING comfort in the afterlife, was found in horizontal hieroglyphs on the front of the coffin belonging to a man with the name of Khnumhotep (see illus. 62). The coffin is the typical casket type from the Middle Period, painted yellow outside and white inside. The hieroglyphs are blue on a yellow ground.

The three vertical bands of text on the front of the coffin, reading from left to right, describe the deceased as worthy (of protection and care in the afterlife) by the deities Duamutef, Shu, and Imseti. Shu's partner, Tefnut, and the two remaining sons of Horus, Hapy and Qebehsenuef, are named on the reverse side.

The narrowness of the coffin can be explained by the fact that the body was not placed on its back, but leaning on its left shoulder with its back against the side of the coffin. It was only in this position that the deceased could look out through the eyes painted on the coffin's side. In the tomb, the coffin was positioned so that the deceased was looking towards the east, towards the rising sun. According to religious belief, this would have allowed the deceased to see and thereby participate in the sun-god's daily crossing of the sky.

62   Box coffin for Khnumhotep, Middle Kingdom.
Cedar of Lebanon, length: 166 cms.
Probably from Meir, Middle Egypt.
Pelizaeus-Museum, Hildesheim, Inv. 4750

63   Official with staff, Middle Kingdom.
Tomb painting from Beni Hasan

64   Hunting with bows and arrows,
Middle Kingdom.
Tomb painting from Beni Hasan

65   Bird-hunt with throw sticks,
Middle Kingdom.
Tomb painting from Beni Hasan

66 Model of animals being slaughtered, Middle Kingdom.

Painted wood, 23 x 30 x 33 cms.

Probably from Assiut.

Pelizaeus-Museum, Hildesheim, Inv. 1694

Opposite page

67 Tomb statuette of a man, Middle Kingdom.

Painted wood, height: 37 cms.

Pelizaeus-Museum, Hildesheim, Inv. 4565

Magical protection through invocations to guardian gods and the enumeration of offerings were not sufficient to ensure well-being in the afterlife. There also had to be generous funerary equipment, which had to correspond to the deceased's social standing in this world so that it might be replicated in the next. So, for example, high-ranking officials would have their insignia laid in their coffins with them, in certain cases including wooden sceptres (cf. illus. 63).

Other important objects calculated to emphasise the standing of the deceased were weapons, although the bows and arrows found would not only have been used in conflict but would also have been used for hunting animals such as antelopes, wild cattle, and lions (see illus. 64). These bows were generally made of native acacia or tamarisk wood, while the arrows were usually made from reeds with flint heads.

Wild fowl were hunted using throw-sticks, and in many tomb illustrations showing fowling parties the deceased is seen standing in a papyrus boat with a throw-stick in his hand (see illus. 65).

Another element of funerary equipment was a statue of the deceased. During the Middle Kingdom, these were often small-scale wooden statuettes which sometimes were included in the coffin. They may be seen as a kind of 'substitute' body so that the soul would always have somewhere to live even if the mummy were damaged.

The tomb statuette in illustration 67 represents a man with very short black hair holding a papyrus roll in his hand. He was certainly an official, probably a scribe. He is dressed in a white garment reaching down to his calves and knotted below his right shoulder. The offering prayer written on the front of the garment is incomplete and does not give the name of the deceased.

During the Middle Kingdom, funerary equipment also included wooden models of ships and workshops. They were meant to guarantee that the deceased should be mobile and well provided for in the afterlife. There are models of textile workshops where linen is being spun and woven, and of workshops where wheat is being made into bread and ale. Frequently, these models might also show cattle being brought in, slaughtered, and butchered, as well as meat being handled thereafter. In the small model from Hildesheim shown in illustration 66, a bound cow lies on a wooden board on the ground. A dark stain on its neck shows that the animal has already been slaughtered by having an artery cut. The slaughterer, still holding a knife in his hand, bends over the animal. Mounted on the same base are other small figures: a scribe with a writing block and three other men.

Lavish funerary equipment is also found in women's tombs, with finely worked mirrors and cosmetic jars demonstrating the status of the deceased.

As we have seen, embalming techniques were not yet fully developed during the Middle Kingdom. Bodies from that period are barely intact today, because muscle and skin were generally not well enough preserved. Roughly a dozen mummies from this period survive in museums outside Egypt. Typical of mummies of the Middle Kingdom are the vast quantities of linen cloths and strips that were used to wrap them,

68   The mummy of Inemakhet, Middle Kingdom.

Length: 190 cms.

From Abusir.

Ägyptisches Museum, Berlin, Inv. 16201

69   Three dimensional reconstruction of the skull of Inemakhet

creating 'sausage-shaped' forms. One mummy was found to have been wrapped in 440 square yards (375 square metres) of linen.

A good example of a mummy from the Middle Kingdom is that of Inemakhet, which was recently examined in Berlin (see illus. 68). Since the body tissues have not been preserved and the body cavities were not refilled, the bones have to a certain extent worked loose. The mummy is wrapped in large amounts of linen with a long chain of rounded faience beads underneath the last layer, although the thread they were strung on has disintegrated. The mummy was finished with a protective mask of painted linen cartonnage that sits on the mummy's shoulders, its face further up than that of the deceased (see illus. 69). The carefully prepared and wrapped body of Inemakhet was buried in a shaft tomb in the tomb complex of King Nyuserra in Abusir, along with his insignia of office, a statuette, and other funerary goods.

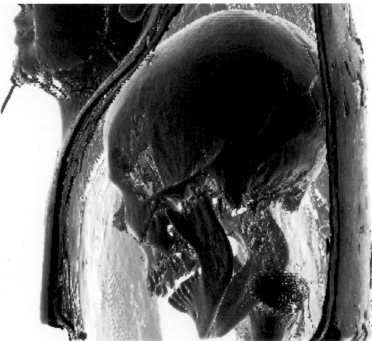

THREE COFFINS FOR ONE MUMMY

ACCORDING TO INSCRIPTIONS ON HIS COFFIN, PENIU, WHO lived around 800 B.C., was a guard in the temple of Min in Akhmim. His title clearly indicates a high office in the priesthood, the same one his father, Djedkhonsiuefankh, had held before him. Peniu or his family must have been immensely wealthy to afford his lavish tomb and no less than three coffins.

The sleek wooden outer coffin matches the mummy in shape (see illus. 70). Today, it is black in colour, but originally it was painted with a gold pigment and must have looked splendid. This outer coffin enclosed an intermediate coffin, also made of wood, but with a fine coating of painted plaster (see illus. 71). The idealised face, framed by a long, straight wig, does not reveal whether this coffin was intended for a male or female occupant. Flowers crown the wig, and a floral collar is painted on the chest. Between the two sides of the wig and on a white ground, there is a depiction of Osiris with Isis.

The images and the text below the elongated hieroglyphs and the winged sun-disc describe the judgement which everyone had to undergo before joining the ranks of the 'justified'. The course of this judgement 'reads' from the bottom end of the coffin upwards. The four lowest registers comprise the so-called negative confessions. Forty crouched, human- and animal-headed judges accuse Peniu of various sins. He responds with a declaration of innocence that always follows the same pattern: 'Hail, Lord of Truth, who comest forth from Maati, I have not stolen.' The sins under consideration are of different kinds, ranging from murder and grave robbery to falsifying corn measures.

But Peniu's protestations of innocence are not enough on their own. His statements are further tested by the weighing of his heart. This part of the proceedings is shown in the centre of the coffin. Peniu, already mummified, stands to the right. His heart lies on the left side of the scales and is being weighed against a feather, the symbol of truth. Below the scales crouches the jackal-headed god Anubis, here in his role as Keeper of the Balance, watching to see what the outcome will be. The animal-like, composite creature below and to the right of the scales with a knife in its paw is 'the Gobbler'. The god Thoth, in the shape of an baboon, waits to record the result of the weighing, holding a quill and a writing block at the ready. The whole process is observed by Maat, the goddess of truth, recognisable by the feather on her head.

70   Outer coffin belonging to Peniu,

Third Intermediate Period, c. 800 B.C.

Length: 203 cms.

Probably from Akhmim.

Pelizaeus-Museum, Hildesheim, Inv. 1902a

Of course, Peniu is judged favourably by the tribunal of the dead, and so he is seen 'justified' in the last register. He wears a long white garment and is led towards Osiris, the judge of the dead, by the falcon-headed god Horus. Osiris sits on a throne in a pavilion with the four sons of Horus before him. The inside of the base of the coffin is decorated with the figure of Osiris and *djed* pillars. In the centre is the customary prayer to Osiris with the plea for offerings of food.

This intermediate coffin contains yet another coffin made of linen cartonnage rather than wood (see illus. 72). This kind of casing was made round a mould, and when it was finished, slit open down the back, so that the mummy could be placed inside it. The slit would then be closed up again by lacing narrow strips of linen through small holes.

Peniu's face on the cartonnage case is painted black, as is his wig. Black was the colour of silt from the Nile and so, associated with re-generation, became the colour of Osiris and symbolised rebirth. At the chin on the cartonnage case, there is a ceremonial beard of woven wood. The entire top of the case is richly decorated with painted mythological scenes. Above the feet, the mummy is shown lying on a bier, watched over by the jackal-headed god Anubis. Two goddesses, one on either side of the bier, give the mummy an *ankh*. In the register above this is another depiction of the judgement ceremony, this time with the god Ra-Horakhty presiding. The scene below, showing Osiris between two trees, is a symbol of regeneration after death. Under a winged sun-disc, Peniu is taken from the god Thoth to Osiris, before whom stand the four sons of Horus on a lotus blossom.

The extremely careful 'packing' of Peniu is matched by the em-balming of his body. The mummy is still in its cartonnage case today. Originally, it was wrapped in a net of faience beads, but the threads have largely disintegrated so that the beads now lie loose on the mummy. In 1975, this mummy was examined using conventional X-ray techniques. It became clear that Peniu had lived at least into his fifth decade. Because his skeleton does not show any degeneration, he was probably not more than fifty years old, however. His teeth are also in remarkably good condition, although they are significantly worn down (see p. 128).

The appearance of Peniu's mummy can be deduced from that of Tadithorpara, who was buried in Akhmim at around the same time or a little later (see illus. 73). This mummy is covered with a net of tubular and flat blue faience beads. A winged scarab, also made of faience beads, is sewn to the chest area, like the similarly made sons of Horus below it, although only three of them have survived. The scarab and the sons of Horus are all there to protect the mummy.

The outer linen directly underneath the beads looks a natural colour now, but chemical tests have shown that it was originally coloured red with dye from the safflower plant, although only a few traces of this light-sensitive red are still to be found in the folds of the fabric. The entire mummy is wrapped in one cloth secured by strips of natural linen running lengthwise, crosswise, and diagonally. With the red of the cloth, the beige strips of linen, and the blue net of beads, the mummy must have been marvellously colourful when it was completed.

71   Middle coffin belonging to Peniu,

Third Intermediate Period, c. 800 B.C.

Length: 182 cms.

Probably from Akhmim.

Pelizaeus-Museum, Hildesheim, Inv. 1902b

Opposite page

72   Cartonnage case for Peniu,

Third Intermediate Period, c. 800 B.C.

Length: 176 cms.

Probably from Akhmim.

Pelizaeus-Museum, Hildesheim, Inv. 1902c

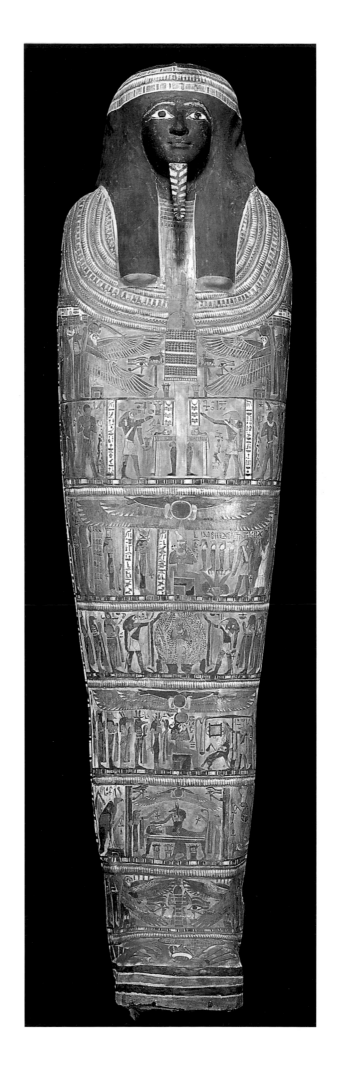

the sky-goddess, Nut, and a scarab spread their wings protectively. The next gilded field shows the mummy standing upright with several deities, and the last depicts it lying on a lion-shaped bier, with Anubis holding an embalming jug and indicating that the embalming has been carried out correctly. To the right and left of the bier are the grieving figures of Isis and Nephthys.

The foot section of the cartonnage case is particularly extravagant with its three-dimensional feet and sandal straps. The toe-nails are gilded, and there are two heavy foot rings around the ankles.

At the edge of the middle section, there is a small inscription, which must be a kind of note or label specific to that mummy. It names Hor as the deceased as well as his father, Petemine, and his grandfather Petharwer. It is written in demotic script, as was customary in Egypt at that time; demotic script was used for administrative, legal, and business purposes. In matters of religion, hieroglyphs and their cursive variant, hieratic script, continued to be used.

78   Mummy decorations for Hor, Ptolemaic, c. 100 B.C.

Length: 175 cms.

From Hawara.

Ägyptisches Museum, Berlin, Inv. 13463

EGYPT UNDER ROMAN RULE

IN 30 B. C., THE COMBINED FORCES OF ANTONY AND CLEOPATRA, the last Ptolemaic queen, were vanquished by Octavius, who later became Emperor Caesar Augustus. After Antony and Cleopatra committed suicide, Octavius took possession of Egypt. The country was now administered by Roman prefects and under the direct command of the Roman emperors, who were regarded in Egypt as pharaohs. They built temples in the valley of the Nile, placed images of themselves as pharaohs in these buildings, and accepted the veneration of the people. Large numbers of Romans now lived in Egypt: officials of the administration, soldiers in military installations, and legionaries who had settled there. They all influenced Egyptian culture, and changes were particularly evident in funeral rituals.

Nevertheless, a sizeable number of mummy cases continued to be worked in the traditional Egyptian manner, as is exemplified by a cartonnage case recently restored by the Museum für Kunst und Gewerbe, Hamburg (see pp. 133 ff.). The faces of the masks were usually still gilded, and the eyes and eyebrows were often inlaid with coloured glass. Several separate sections of painted cartonnage were used to encase mummies, and either the feet were given cartonnage soles or both feet were put together into a so-called mummy shoe.

Evidence of the costs involved in mummification and burial have come down to us from the Roman period. The most expensive items were the mask — at a cost of 64 drachmas — and the embalming materials such as wax, fat, oils, embalming oils, myrrh, and ochre — coming to a total of 65 drachmas. Bearing in mind that at this time, a worker would normally earn about 30 drachmas a month, it is clear that a properly prepared mummy was costly and certainly not within everyone's grasp. So the less well-off could not afford cartonnage cases at all and only small quantities of embalming oils.

During the Roman period, as before during the Ptolemaic Period, cartonnage mummy cases were not only produced using plaster-reinforced linen. Another method was to use pressed papyri stuck together in layers — old documents often served this purpose. Since it is now possible to separate the layers of papyrus and read them, these papyri have become a valuable source of information about the administration of Egypt during the Graeco-Roman period. At the beginning of this century, material of this kind took on such importance for Egyptology that several archaeological expeditions were sent to Egypt specifically in order to collect papyrus cartonnage. The traditional Egyptian style of funerary masks changed under Roman rule, however. Up until and throughout the Ptolemaic Period, masks depicted the deceased as deified, with an idealised face. Now, suddenly, signs of individuality appeared — above all in the hair and in beards, clothes, and jewellery, either painted on or formed in plaster. In addition, mouths were now seen to smile, in a manner distinctly reminiscent of Archaic Greek statues.

The techniques used to wrap mummies also changed in Roman times. The outer layer was often made of narrow, often coloured strips of linen woven into an intricate pattern of squares. Sometimes, a gilded button might even be fastened in the centre of each square. Less attention was paid to the effectiveness of the preservation process itself. In many cases, the most skilful of wrappings may contain an extremely badly preserved mummy.

In Middle Egypt at this time, a particular kind of individually worked funerary mask was developed. A mixture of sand, clay, carboniferous chalk, and plaster was pressed into a mould. Hair, jewellery, and so on were worked separately and added to the mask. These plaster masks have a breastplate made of plaster or wood that extends downwards into the wrappings so that the mask would have been held firmly in place. Unfortunately, no mummies have survived with this kind of mask still in position, because masks were removed for sale beginning at the end of the last century.

The plaster masks of the Roman period differ not only in material but also in position from earlier examples. Whereas classical Egyptian funerary masks lay flat on the face of the deceased, now the head was half raised up and showed the deceased at the moment of awakening to new life.

Most of the plaster masks held in museums today were found in the burial ground in the old town of Hermopolis in Middle Egypt. Unfortunately, the early explorers did not record details about the burial grounds themselves, which means that the dating of these masks almost entirely depends on stylistic variations such as the way the hair and beard were worn. For example, the mask of a woman with three rows of corkscrew curls on her forehead and three locks of hair behind her ears is thought to have come from the second century A.D. (see illus. 79), and the plaster mask of a man with curled hair, side-whiskers, and beard most probably comes from the same time (see illus. 80).

The mummy of a young girl (see illus. 81) is a striking example of the merging of ancient Egyptian and Roman notions of death. This is the only mummy of its kind to have survived intact. Since the child was so small, it was not a matter of securing a mask on a breastplate. Instead, the entire mummy was covered in a layer of plaster about half an inch (1–1.5 centimetres) thick. There is no mistaking the half-raised head in the moment of awakening after death. The hair consists of fine curls, and the large eyes made of glass look very lifelike. Around her neck, the girl wears a golden chain with a pendant, with further items of jewellery modelled in plaster: rings on her fingers and golden arm- and ankle bands. She is dressed in a red, coat-like garment.

Of particular interest are the objects that the girl is holding in her hands. In her left hand is a small dove. According to Graeco-Roman understanding, this was a symbol of the goddess Aphrodite-Venus. It has been found on Egyptian gravestones from the Roman period and just occasionally on the plaster masks of children who died young. Perhaps the image of the dove was meant to secure love for the child in the next world.

Opposite page

79   Plaster mask of a woman, 2nd century A.D.

Height: 26 cms. Probably from Hermopolis.

Pelizaeus-Museum, Hildesheim, Inv. 573

80   Plaster mask of a man, 2nd century A.D.

Height: 26 cms. Probably from Hermopolis.

Pelizaeus-Museum, Hildesheim, Inv. 4566

81   The mummy of a child in a plaster coffin, probably 2nd century A.D..

Length: 67 cms.

Pelizaeus-Museum, Hildesheim, Inv. LH 14

The object in the girl's right hand is very much a part of Egyptian tradition. Minimal traces of red show that, despite the somewhat angular shape, this is a posy of rose blossoms of the kind often found on cartonnage cases from the Roman period. It symbolises the 'wreath of justification' that the deceased would receive from Osiris, having passed the Judgement of the Dead.

The plaster casing completely encloses the mummy of the child, so it was only possible to discover the condition of the body by using X-rays (see illus. 82 – 84). They showed that the mummy is in very good condition, although a break in the knee area of the now-restored plaster case had somewhat damaged the legs. The girl's body is 22 inches (56 centimetres) in length. According to present-day rates of growth in Europe, one would assume this to be an infant, but in Egypt at that time both adults and children were much smaller. Adult mummies of men and women are frequently less than 5 feet 2 inches (1.60 metres) in length. So this child, in view also of her fully formed milk teeth, must have died when she was at least two years old.

CT scans show the techniques used in this mummification. The brain was removed through a hole in the nape of the neck, causing a small piece of bone to break off which is still visible lying inside the skull. At the place where this breakage occurred, some of the linen used for wrapping the mummy came through the hole into the skull. It is not impossible that there may still be a certain amount of dehydrated brain tissue at this point. At the back of the mummy, running from the head to halfway down the back, three palm-leaf spines were incorporated into the wrappings in order to lend strength to the tiny body. The embalmers removed the viscera through an incision in the abdominal wall above the pelvis on the left side as was usual. Since the body was not refilled with linen or sawdust, the chest and abdomen were flattened by the wrappings. The X-rays did not reveal any pathological abnormalities which might have given a clue as to the reason for the death of this young child.

Plaster mask

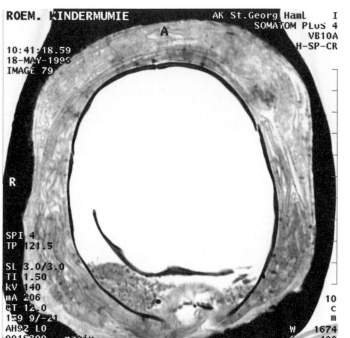

Plaster case

Linen wrappings

Skull

Broken fragment
of skull

Plaster case
Linen wrappings

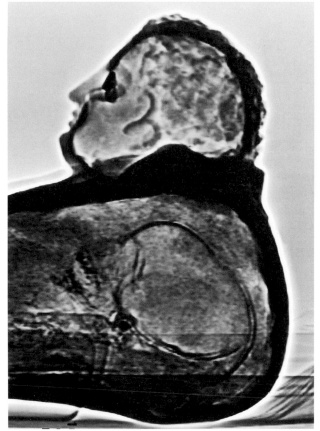

Skull

82   CT scan of the head section of the mummy of a child
(see illus. 81)

83   CT scan of the head

84   CT scan of the shoulder area

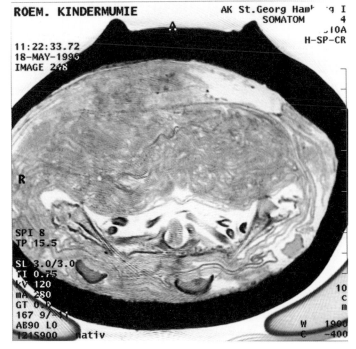

Plaster case

Linen wrappings

Bones from
shoulder blades
and upper ribs

Spines incorporated
in wrappings

MUMMY PORTRAITS —
ONLY IN ROMAN EGYPT

ROMAN INFLUENCES ON MUMMIFICATION WERE EVEN more critical in Fayum, a large oasis lying approximately 45 miles (70 kilometres) south-west of present-day Cairo. During the Middle Kingdom, the pharaohs built their pyramids there — Senusret II in Lahun and Amenemhat III in Hawara. Greek writers describing the extended burial temple belonging to the pyramid of Amenemhat III referred to it as a labyrinth. During the Graeco-Roman period, Fayum was densely populated, and people used the old structures and surrounding areas as cemeteries because they were held to be specially sacred.

In 1887, the necropolis at Fayum suddenly became of interest to antiquities collectors. Interest developed at the eastern edge of a nearby oasis called Er-Rubayat when local inhabitants found a large number of mummies that included a portrait of the deceased in the head-piece. Unlike the mummies of pharaonic times, these were individual likenesses. Their style was clearly influenced by that of Roman portraiture, and they gave the impression that the mummy was looking out of the case directly at the viewer. This was no doubt intentional on the part of the portrait artist, because at the time they were made, mummies were not buried immediately, but were kept upright in a special place, presumably a cupboard-like shrine. It was only when the mummy ceased to be of interest to the family that it would be stacked without a coffin along with other mummies in a simple, tiled trench.

Research regarding these portraits indicates that they do not always show the person at the age when they died. On the contrary, these likenesses were most probably painted at a time when the subjects felt that they were at their best. The portraits were then stored for use after death. Of course, the expense involved was considerable. During his excavations at Hawara, the English Egyptologist Flinders Petrie established that only one in a hundred mummies would be a portrait mummy. Today, we know of more than 750.

These likenesses made during the subject's lifetime were painted on cypress, lime, or cedar boards not more than a sixteenth of an inch (a few millimetres) thick. Mineral dyes and two different kinds of binding agents were used.

The portrait of the woman in illustration 85 is painted in wax paints (encaustic) which produce shining colours. The binding agent consists of beeswax mixed with olive oil and resin. The portrait shows a woman with an intricate hair-do, earrings, and two strings of large beads. She wears a red chiton. At the lower edge of the portrait, which has only survived in part, there are clearly identifiable traces of resinous embalming oils that were used in the mummification process.

The portrait of a youth (see illus. 86), on the other hand, was painted in tempera, which produces a much duller surface. In this case, the binding agent was a mixture of water and egg whites. The subject wears

Opposite page

85   Mummy portrait of a woman,
early 4th century A.D.
Encaustic painted wood,
height: 36 cms.
From Er–Rubbiyat.
Museum für Kunst und Gewerbe,
Hamburg, Inv. 1928.42

86   Mummy portrait of a youth,
mid 3rd century A.D.
Tempera painted wood,
height: 30.5 cms.
From Er–Rubbiyat.
Museum für Kunst und Gewerbe,
Hamburg, Inv. 1928.43

'BECOMING OSIRIS'

THE DESIRE TO BECOME ONE WITH OSIRIS AFTER DEATH IS particularly evident in the painted mummy cloths from the Roman period. According to legend, Osiris was killed and torn into pieces by his brother. His wife-sister, Isis, searched untiringly to collect his remains until she was able to bury his body. Since his body was whole again, Osiris could be reanimated and gained eternal life, becoming the king of the dead in the underworld. Eternal life was what everyone wanted to achieve. This process of transfiguration (discussed in greater detail below; see illus. 94 ff.) is illustrated in paintings of the deceased having become Osiris, on mummy cloths, which were laid directly onto the mummy and fastened with narrow linen bindings.

The cloth shown in illustration 92 dates from the last years of pharaonic culture, probably from the second century A.D. Osiris's symbols of power are much changed: instead of a crook and a palm frond, he holds two palm fronds in his hand, with stems that are much too thin and drawn as a line of tiny dots. Two falcons' heads, which normally would form the clasps on large pieces of jewellery or floral collars, are painted on his shoulders, thus bereft of their original meaning and completely misunderstood. Instead of the customary *atef* crown, Osiris wears the regal headcloth (*nemes*) of a pharaoh, although somewhat diminished in size. Around his neck he has a gold collar set with large stones. Unfortunately, only the lower half of the portrait of the deceased-as-Osiris has survived, but it is clearly individualistic. Two goddesses with cows' horns and a sun-disc on their heads stand to his left and right. Dressed in colourful garments, they obviously represent the sisters of Osiris, Isis and Nephthys, now protecting the dead 'Osiris' as they once protected their brother.

The body of Osiris is in the shape of a mummy and covered with a brightly painted net of beads. Only his hands are showing, and his feet are uncovered. He stands in a papyrus boat sailing by the banks of the River Nile. But the plants are not the traditional blue or white lotuses (*Nymphaea coerula* and *Nymphea lotus*). Instead, they have the lifelike leaves and pink flowers of the Indian lotus (*Nelumbo nucifer*), which was in fact not established in Egypt until the sixth century B.C. On either side of the feet are goat-sphinxes in a gesture of prayer. The four sons of Horus are also represented, two on either side. On the left are Imseti and Hapy, on the right are Duamutef and Qebehsenuef. Although there are no explanatory inscriptions, they are easily recognisable by their characteristic heads.

The deceased is not only shown on the cloth as Osiris, but also in a small image to the right of the Osiris figure. This scene is a vivid example of old motifs being reworked during the Roman period in a new style. In the tomb and coffin paintings of earlier times, Nut, the tree-goddess, is often shown reaching down from her tree, giving water in a *hes* vase to the deceased or the deceased's soul-bird. This delicately painted

Opposite page

91 Mummy cloth, detail
(see illus. 92)

91 Mummy cloth, 3rd century A.D.
Painted linen, 169 x 107 cms.
Pelizaeus–Museum, Hildesheim,
Inv. LH 3

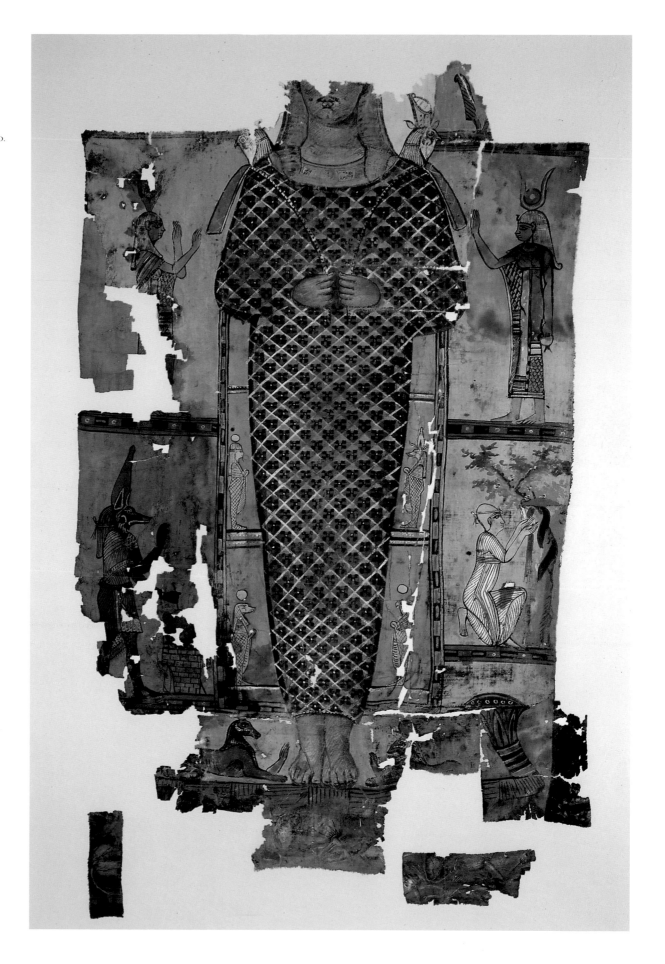

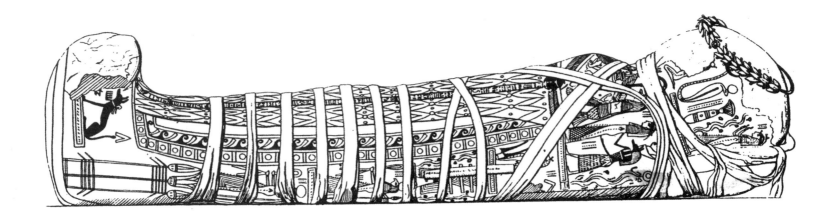

scene also has a tree, albeit with many branches and with red and white flowers, but now there is no goddess, and the *hes* vase has become a spindle bottle. The deceased is seen kneeling, wearing a finely pleated garment, holding his hands out to water. On his head, he wears a blue wig or a cap with a headband.

On the other side of the Osiris figure, in the corresponding position, there is a very unusual image of the jackal-headed Anubis wearing a brightly coloured garment. On his head, he bears the crown of Upper Egypt, although it is red instead of the customary white and inclines forwards instead of backwards. Anubis's left hand is raised in a gesture of worship while with the right he stirs something in a pot over a fire. Most likely, embalming oils are being heated here for use in the preparation of a mummy.

The exceptionally finely painted images on this cloth show ancient Egyptian iconography in a distinctly Roman style.

THE DECLINE OF THE EMBALMER'S ART

IN THE SECOND CENTURY A.D., THE EGYPTIANS STILL sometimes made coffins with painted decorations that restated their traditional religious beliefs. People seem to have felt the need to record the things that mattered to them. This same need had produced richly decorated temples with extensive inscriptions in the days of the Ptolemies. At the same time, however, stylistic decline was all too evident, and elements of Greek mythology were already finding their way into Egyptian religion. The advent of Christianity in Egypt did not mean that the population simply discarded their earlier beliefs. In fact, they introduced some of the old traditions into the new religion. The Church fathers rejected the notion of embalming in no uncertain terms, however. The bodies of the dead should return to dust; a pure soul was all that was needed for eternal life.

95 Cartonnage case for Paynakht,
c. 100 A.D.
Length: 136 cms. From Akhmim.
Ägyptisches Museum, Berlin,
Inv. 14291

Opposite page
93 Mummy of Petemenophis,
2nd century A.D.
Showing mummy with mummy cloth.

94 Cartonnage case for Paynakht
(left-hand side).

THE MUMMY CASE OF
THE BOY PAYNAKHT

THE COFFIN BELONGING TO PAYNAKHT IS AN IMPRESSIVE
document of the end of ancient Egyptian culture. The cartonnage case
must have been magnificent (see illus. 94 ff.). This included a bier,
although only fragments of it were found. Although the mummy is
missing, the size of the cartonnage case indicates that Paynakht was only
a boy when he died.

The sequence and distribution of the scenes, motifs, and short texts
were carefully chosen and matched. The conventional notions expressed
in the images rub shoulders with new concepts of the afterlife, death,
and resurrection just as one might expect from the case's late date. In this
respect, the face is particularly striking: the head is slightly raised up out
of the wrappings, the eyes are open, the mouth is opened as if about to
speak, and the open nostrils evoke the act of breathing as the symbol of

the renewed gift of life — life in the next world, that is. Although illustrating the process in this way was new, the ideas derived from the so-called Coffin Texts of two thousand years earlier.

As far as subject matter is concerned the decoration is on two levels: the earthly and the divine. Running round both sides of the body and taking in the feet, earthly matters are represented by a frieze of semi-abstract houses, boldly executed with a broad brush, while the divine is shown as the world of the gods, the next world. This is symbolised by ten deities seated to the right and left, who clearly have their origins in the traditional concept of the forty-two assessor-gods. They all carry the emblem of Maat in their hands, symbolising justice and recalling Maat's duty to accompany the deceased through the process of the Judgement of the Dead in the hall of Osiris. The ten judges are evidently an allusion to Chapter 125 of *The Book of the Dead*, where the Judgement of the Dead is described in words and images (see pp. 41 ff.).

On the left side of the body, there is an abbreviated reference to events in the next world: after judgement by the gods, the mummy of the deceased, mourned by the goddesses Isis and Nephthys at its head

and feet, is transported on a barge along the waterways that lead into the next world. Symbols of salvation such as the seated phoenix and the scarab in a circle precede the deceased on two more barges accompanied by the Anubis-jackal. This scene is drawn from the illustrations in the *Amduat, The Book of What Is in the Underworld*, which was found only in the tombs of kings in earlier times. Here as elsewhere, fifteen hundred years of cult activity were modified by democracy: as the scarab in the circle was to become the rising sun, so also the king — and now ordinary mortals too — would be reborn. However, the sequence of pictures demonstrates that this point had not yet been reached. The barge with the mummy, the phoenix, and the self-regenerating sun-god are only stages on the journey to the final goal. In front of the barge, there is still the god Bes holding a snake and a large key. Bes was in fact a folk god whose duty it was to protect people at critical times in their lives — for example, at birth. Bes's protective powers are clear from the way he holds tightly onto the snake-demons that are often shown guarding the entrance to the next world. Here, he is protecting the boy Paynakht from their evil. The keys relate to a different aspect of the god. During

his long career, he was equated with Shu, god of the air, who was known as the bearer of the heavenly spheres. As a god of the heavens, it made sense that he too should receive the keys to heaven, which Greek influence had ascribed to Anubis and which would open the way into the next world.

It was only with the approval and protection of the god Bes that the deceased could 'become' Osiris and share in his immortality — following the pattern laid down in the distant mythological past. This scene is placed directly below the deceased's head. Entwined to the right and the left of the god, who turns towards the deceased, is a snake. This is Uroborus, the *mehen* snake, whose role in the *Amduat* is to guard the transformation of the old evening sun-god into the youthful morning sun.

As to the Osirian Paynakht, his head is protected by a blue wig, as befits a god (see illus. 95). On this wig is the symbol of Abydos, the holy site associated with the resurrection of Osiris. A broad collar lies on Paynakht's chest and shoulders. The material descending on both sides in generous folds seems more like a garment than the shroud it is. Having been resurrected, Paynakht carries the crook and scourge, the regalia of Osiris.

The sequence of the scenes on the right side of the body matches that on the left. First, there are ten gods, then another procession of three barges approaching the god Bes. This is no doubt a reference to an ancient cult practice: the journey of the deceased as a statue and as a mummy to Abydos. In the first barge, there is a canopic shrine, while the second contains the mummified corpse protected by the goddesses Isis and Nephthys as female vultures. In the third barge, watched over by Isis (to its head) and Nephthys (to its feet), there is a seated statue with an Osiris crown and a beard that might be worn by a god.

The foot section has its own special embellishment. The feet, in sandals, are enclosed in a small temple decorated with a uraeus frieze. But in order to retain at least something of the traditional elements of such 'mummy shoes', there are depictions of two 'enemies' on either side of the foot section, representing demons that the deceased is treading underfoot.

The main interest of Paynakht's case is without a doubt the view of the body from above. In the centre is the resurrected Paynakht framed by the lotus of eternity and two *wadjet* eyes (see illus. 97). An inscription on the centre of the figure tells us that this is the Osirian Paynakht, the justified; the gods are invoked to see to his offerings. The scene is like a precious, safflower-red-dyed shroud painted onto the case. Indeed, the effect of the painting is of precious materials.

The head and chest sections were worked separately and gilded, as were the other areas of skin. The face must also have been gilded. Both hands are visible. The right one straightens the chiton, the dress of the living. The slightly raised head is striking for its straight fringe, typical for the time. A wreath in Paynakht's hair (the wreath of the justified) lends dignity to his face.

A female vulture, either Isis or Nephthys, protects the back of the head, as was the custom on separately worked funerary masks. The em-phasis on the head by means of a mask, or here as part of the cartonnage case, must relate to the notion of the head as the seat of life.

Individual scenes are bordered by narrow inscriptions, one of which includes the name of Paynakht's mother, Senefnebmerut. As well as the customary wish for offerings, there is also an illustration of a theological notion which is found on other coffins and cartonnage cases of the period, namely that the soul belongs in heaven while the body is tied to the earth.

This cartonnage case brings together contemporary and traditional elements. The winged Bes with the keys to heaven may represent the Hellenistic adoption of an earlier Greek myth concerning a god with the keys to Hades. This may have served in turn as the precursor of the Christian notion of death and resurrection (St Peter with his keys comes to mind). The individual parts of the cartonnage case, particularly the face, show that Egyptian and non-Egyptian believers clearly felt the need to translate their understanding of resurrection into images.

H.K.

II

ANCIENT EGYPTIAN MUMMIES IN EUROPE — FROM MEDICAL REMEDY TO SOCIETY PASTIME

THE EGYPTIAN ART OF EMBALMING HAS BEEN KNOWN TO the West since antiquity. The Christian church, however, only approved of embalming for especially holy personages or for holders of its highest offices, rejecting the process as a sinful expression of human vanity for ordinary believers. This meant that as time passed, Egyptian mummies came to be seen as the relics of a heathen culture.

THE LÜBECK APOTHECARIES' MUMMY

Mummies have become goods for trade, Ægypt heals wounds and pharaoh is sold as ointment.

THOMAS BROWN, ENGLISH PHILOSOPHER (1605–1682)

AS EARLY AS THE BEGINNING OF THE MIDDLE AGES, Europeans were already extracting embalming substances from the mummies of ancient Egypt to use as medicines for a range of different illnesses. These extractions were thought of as a decent substitute for the real *moumia*, a bitumen from the Dead Sea and Mesopotamia. But real *moumia* was as expensive as it was hard to find to purchase; it was much simpler to collect the resinous embalming oils that the embalmers of ancient Egypt had poured into mummies' skulls or chest and abdominal cavities. It looked just like *moumia* and was credited with the same healing powers. Over time, the name *moumia* was transferred from bitumen to the embalming substances of ancient Egypt and then to the bodies themselves. Later traders found it too laborious to scratch out the embalming oils, so sections of mummies were simply ground down to powder. As late as 1924, the sales list of a respected German firm of medical suppliers still included 'Mumia vera Aegyptica' at 12 gold marks per kilo.

98   Decorative lid of the Lübeck Apothecaries' Mummy, detail, (cf. illus. 100).

99 Reconstruction of an alchemist's laboratory from the 17th century, with a crocodile mummy hanging from the ceiling.

Germanisches Nationalmuseum, Nürnberg

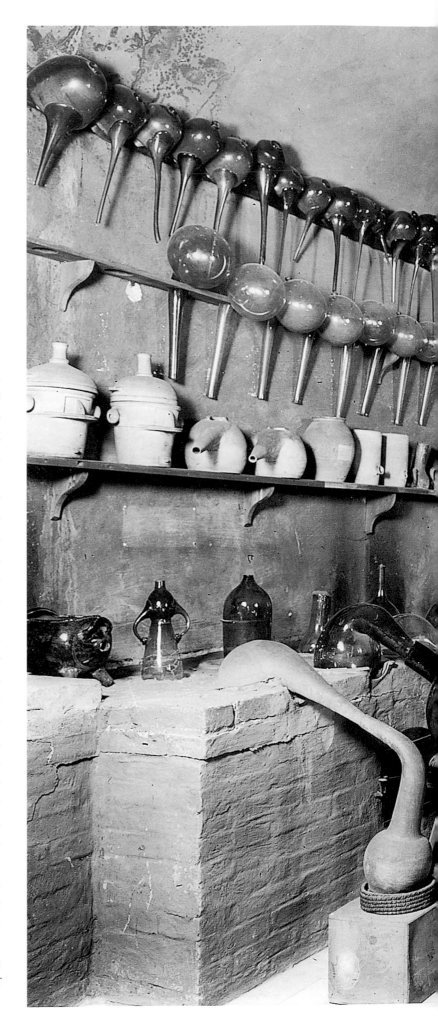

In the Völkerkunde-Sammlung, Lübeck, there is an Egyptian mummy which was once in the possession of the Ratsapotheke in that town. Archival research has shown that as long ago as 1696, it belonged to the town apothecary Jacob Stolterfoht and that it had been restored in 1651, probably already in Lübeck. This makes it the earliest arrival amongst extant mummies in Germany.

The mummy's original coffin and funerary mask had, however, disintegrated during its time in Europe, as had the outermost layer of the linen wrappings. In 1812, therefore, when the Ratsapotheke was closed and the mummy was about to go on exhibition in the town library, a new coffin was made for it, in which the mummy lies to this day. The craftsmen of Lübeck also made a colourful display lid for the coffin and a painted mummy cloth.

Unlike many objects from the period of 'Egyptomania', which developed as a result of Napoleon's campaign in Egypt (see p. 106), neither the display lid nor the mummy cloth are decorated with the usual fantasy hieroglyphs and images. The Lübeck craftsmen took the trouble to decorate both objects by following pictures of the genuine article. The display lid was 'recreated' from an illustration of an Egyptian coffin in a travelogue of 1743 by the English writer Richard Pococke, which is also reproduced in colour in Bertuch's 1795 *Picture Book for Children* (see illus. 101). The coffin is narrower than in Pococke's illustration. The typical long blue Egyptian wig was reinterpreted as a loose-lying head cloth, and the hieroglyphs in a central inscription on the coffin are no longer legible.

The original used for the shroud, which is now kept under glass for conservation reasons, was the picture of a Ptah-Sokar-Osiris statuette published by Athanasius Kircher as early as 1654 (see illus. 104). On the upper section of the shroud is a colourful painted collar of flowers, while on the lower section there is a painted net of beads. Running vertically from the chest to the feet is a pseudo-inscription consisting of real hieroglyphs.

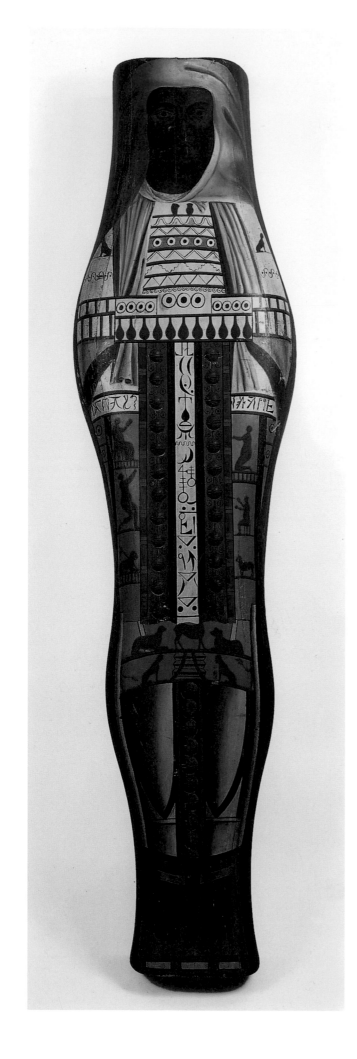

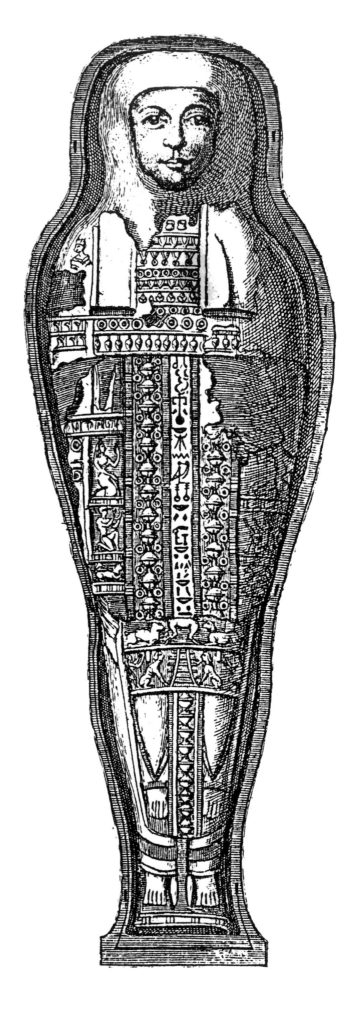

Opposite page

100 Decorative lid of the Lübeck Apothecaries' Mummy
(cf. illus. 103).

101 Illustration of the decorative lid of the Lübeck Apothecaries' Mummy
by Richard Pococke, 1743.

102 From: Friedrich Justin Bertuch, *Altertümer*, 1795.
The image was used when decorating the lid of the Lübeck
Apothecaries' Mummy.

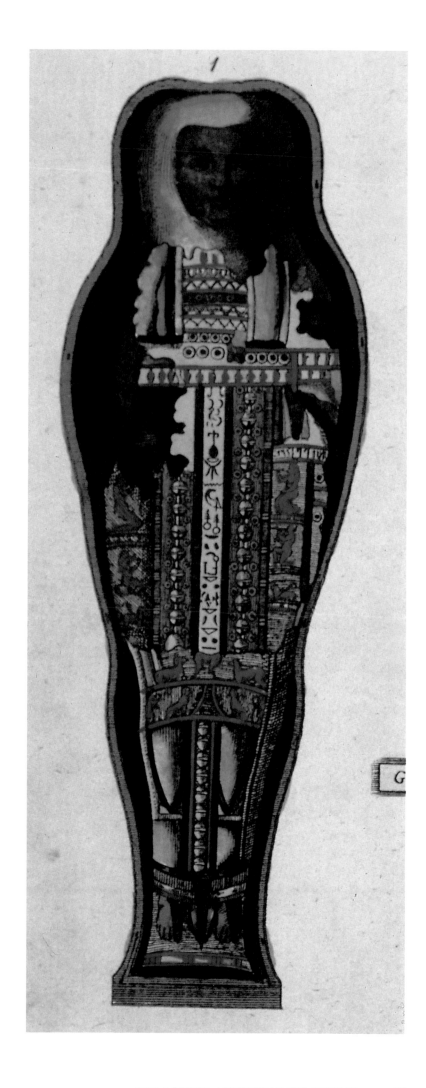

Opposite page

105   X-ray of the thorax
clearly showing the many
amulets.

106   Outlines showing the
distribution of amulets on
the Lübeck Apothecaries'
Mummy.

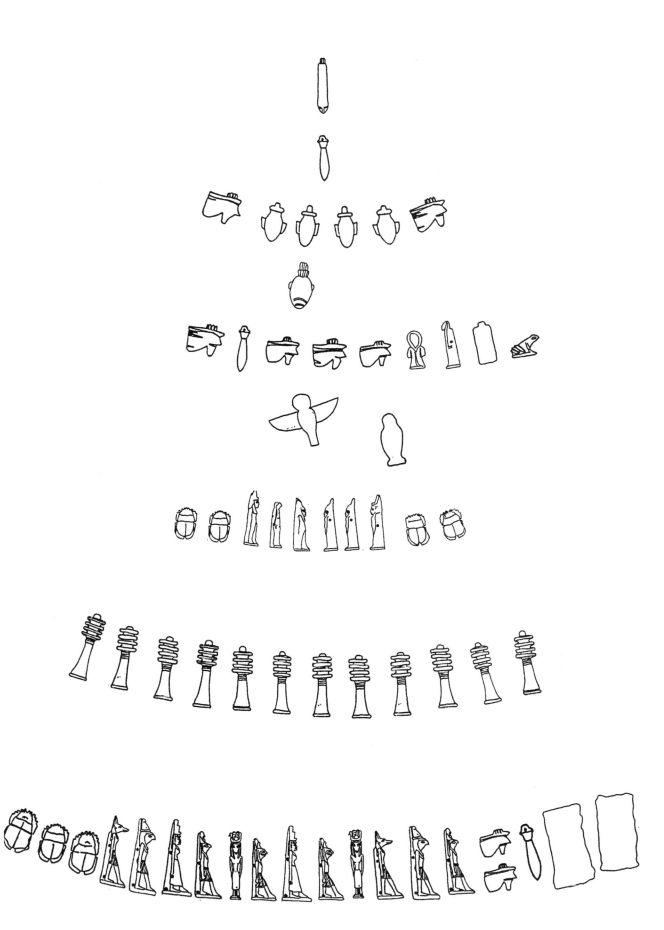

MUMMIES ON THE BILLIARD TABLE

FROM A MILITARY POINT OF VIEW, NAPOLEON'S EGYPTIAN campaign at the turn of the eighteenth century was a fiasco. However, fame and glory were to visit the scientists he took with him to explore Egypt and its culture. They carried out their tasks with outstanding success and published their findings in the many volumes of the richly illustrated *Description de l'Égypte*. A lengthy chapter is devoted to the subject of mummies and includes the first illustrations of mummies' heads — one male and one female (cf. illus. 110). Empress Josephine later received the same female mummy's head as a gift.

In the wake of this enthusiasm, old Egyptian artefacts began to be sought after by collectors. In Egypt, antiquities dealers competed with each other to retrieve objects as quickly as possible from tombs or to remove them from the walls of temples and tombs in order to sell them on the lucrative European art market. The treasures collected at this time formed the basis of the major Egyptian collections in Paris, London, Turin, Leiden, and Berlin. Mummies with their elaborately worked

109   Napoleon looking at a mummy in front of the pyramids, engraving, 19th century

Opposite page

110   Head of female mummy, from an illustration in *Description de l'Égypte*.

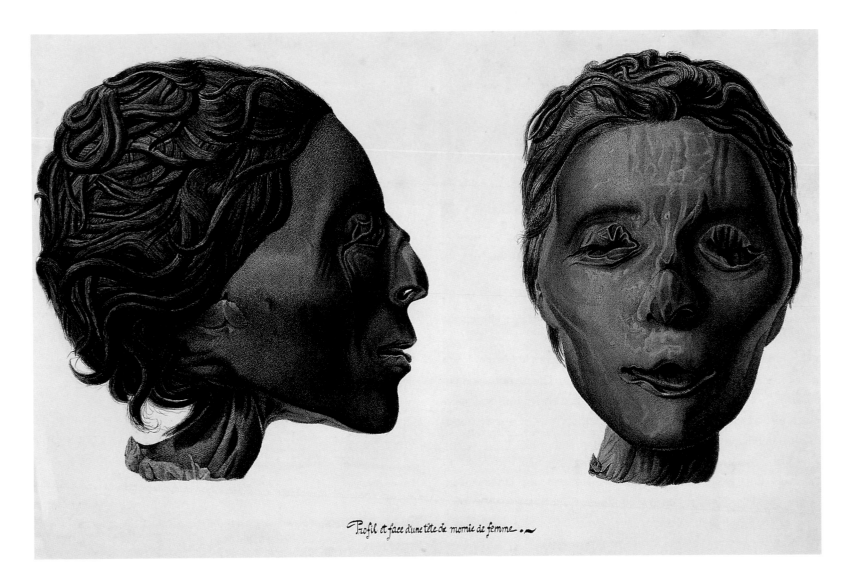

Profil et face d'une tête de momie de femme.

coffins were an important constituent of these collections, and, as publicity for their stocks, dealers would unwrap mummies before an audience. Displays of this nature were put on by Belzoni in London and Cailliaud in Paris, both of whom had large amounts of Egyptiana for sale.

In the nineteenth century, Egypt and the Holy Land were obligatory parts of any young nobleman's Grand Tour. If at all possible, one returned with a mummy as a souvenir. Then, friends would be invited to a fine supper which would be followed by the highpoint of the evening: the unwrapping of the mummy (cf. illus. 112). Those not in a position to undertake a journey to Egypt could still acquire a mummy at auction. But some buyers were badly disappointed when it came to the unwrapping of their costly purchase. Instead of a perfectly preserved human body, there might be a piece of wood, some mummy parts, or, where a child's body might be expected, the mummy of a bird. Fake mummies of this sort were produced by wily, business-conscious dealers using old linen wrappings and pieces of cartonnage (cf. illus. 111).

Today, all major Egyptian collections contain some of these pseudo-mummies, the first of which came onto the market as early as 1771. Some smaller museums did not have the money to buy a mummy, so

they had to fall back on other resources. After the Egyptologist Heinrich Brugsch had given a talk in the north German town of Hamm in 1886, the audience was so enthusiastic that they decided to acquire a mummy for their town. At the time, Emil Brugsch, brother of Heinrich, was a curator at the Egyptian Museum, Cairo, although his main source of income was as an antiquities dealer; many mummies and coffins passed through his hands on their way to European and American museums. The dignitaries of Hamm turned to Emil Brugsch, and, in order to finance their purchase, they founded a Mummy Society and issued shares at 20 marks each (see illus. 113). As a model for the share certificates, the society used a photograph which Emil Brugsch had taken in the museum in Cairo. Down each side of the certificates, there is an image of the coffin of Queen Ahmose-Nefertiry of the 18th Dynasty. This coffin was approximately four yards (4 metres) in length and is on the left-hand side of the original photograph, with the almost identical coffin of Queen Ahmose on the right, although here the two feathers from the crown have not survived. Both of these coffins had been found in the famous royal cache in Deir el-Bahri which had been cleared by a group led by Emil Brugsch in 1881. In the centre at the top of the certificate is an

114 Prince Friedrich-Karl von Hohenzollern in front of the mummy of Ramesses II in the Egyptian Museum in Cairo.
Drawing by Franz Xaver von Garnier, 1883

115 Cartonnage case belonging to Neskhonsupakhered, Late Period c. 500 B.C.
Length: 168 cms.
From Thebes.
Ägyptisches Museum, Berlin, Inv. 8284

Opposite page
116 Poster printed by the Boston bookshop, "The Old Corner Bookstore," on the occasion of the unwrapping of the mummy of Ramesses II, 1887.
Private collection

Uncovering the Mummy of Rameses II., King of Egypt, the Oppressor of the Jews in the Time of Moses.

THE MUMMY OF THE EGYPTIAN KING, RAMESES II., OF THE NINETEENTH DYNASTY (ABOUT 1400 TO 1250 B.C.), STRIPPED OF ITS COVERINGS. FROM PHOTOGRAPHS.

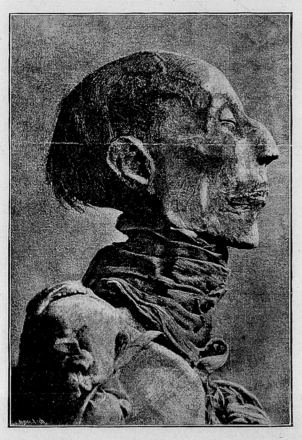

King

Rameses

the

Great.

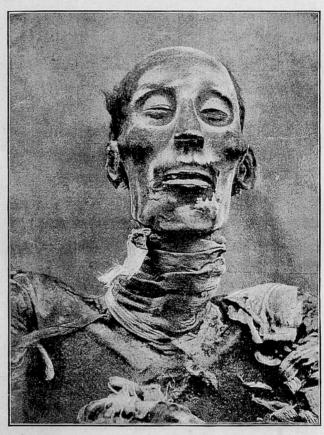

UNCOVERING THE MUMMY OF RAMESES II., KING OF EGYPT, AND OPPRESSOR OF THE JEWS IN THE TIME OF MOSES

PROFESSOR MASPERO'S OFFICIAL REPORT.

BOULAK, June 3, 1886

III. One last wrapper of stiffened canvas, one last winding-sheet of red linen, and then a great disappointment, keenly felt by the operators: the face of the king was covered with a compact mass of bitumen, which completely hid the features. At twenty minutes past eleven, His Highness the Khedive left the Hall of Mummies.

The work was resumed in the afternoon of the same day, and on Thursday morning, as the result of a fresh examination of the bandages revealed inscriptions upon two of them. The first is dated the year IX., the second the year X., of the High Priest Pinotem I. The tarry substance upon the face of the mummy being carefully attacked with the scissors, was detached little by little, and the features became visible. They are less well preserved than those of Rameses II., yet they can to a certain extent be identified with those of the portraits of the conqueror. The head and face are closely shaved, and show no trace of hair or beard. The forehead, without being very lofty or very broad, is better proportioned and more intellectual than that of Rameses II. The brow-ridge is less prominent, the cheekbones are less high, the nose is less hooked, the chin and jaw are less heavy. The eyes appear to be larger, but it is not possible to be certain of this last point, the eyelids having been removed, and the cavities of the eyeballs having been stuffed with rags. The ears are closer to the head than those of Rameses II., and they are pierced in like manner for the reception of earrings. The mouth is disproportionately wide

---

the inscriptions showed that the case had originally been made for a man called Paenmut, 'He who belongs to (the goddess) Mut'. This name had been overpainted with that of a woman, Neskhonsupakhered, 'She who belongs to (the god) Khonsupakhered', although the colour of the face had not been changed. The time of this woman's burial can be put at approximately 500 B.C.

The mummy was taken to Berlin in its cartonnage case and in April 1883, Prince Friedrich-Karl invited his fellow-travellers and other friends to a special occasion at his hunting lodge, Dreilinden. In the newly built billiard room, the mummy from Egypt was laid out on the billiard table. But the eagerly anticipated unwrapping was a sad let-down. Heinrich Brugsch recorded the event:

The brightly painted cartonnage case was opened, the wrappings were undone to reveal before the gaze of the onlookers the brown, perfectly preserved body of a maiden who had departed this earth in the flower of her youth. Not a single amulet, no jewellery, no rolls of papyrus were found with this holy temple virgin. Everyone felt the same sense of disappointment.

The prince gave the case to the Ägyptisches Museum, Berlin, that same year. The mummy's fate is not known.

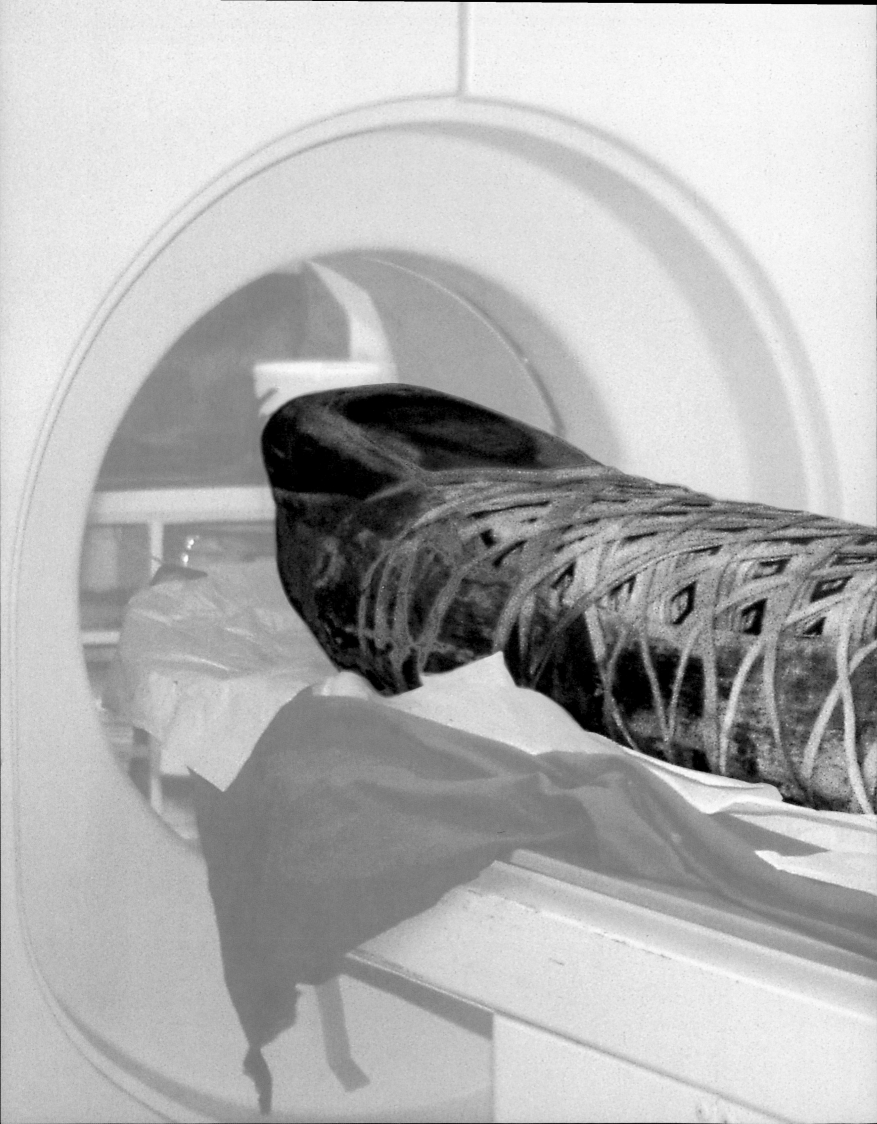

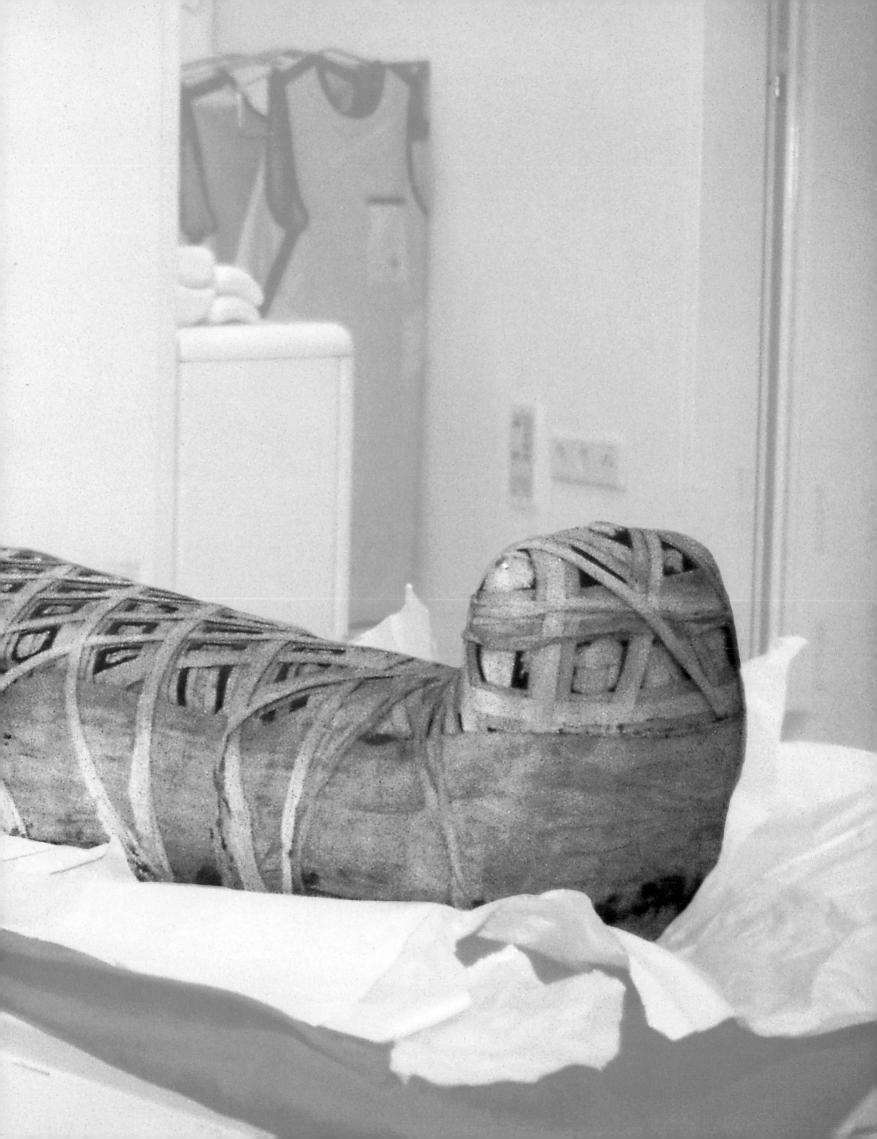

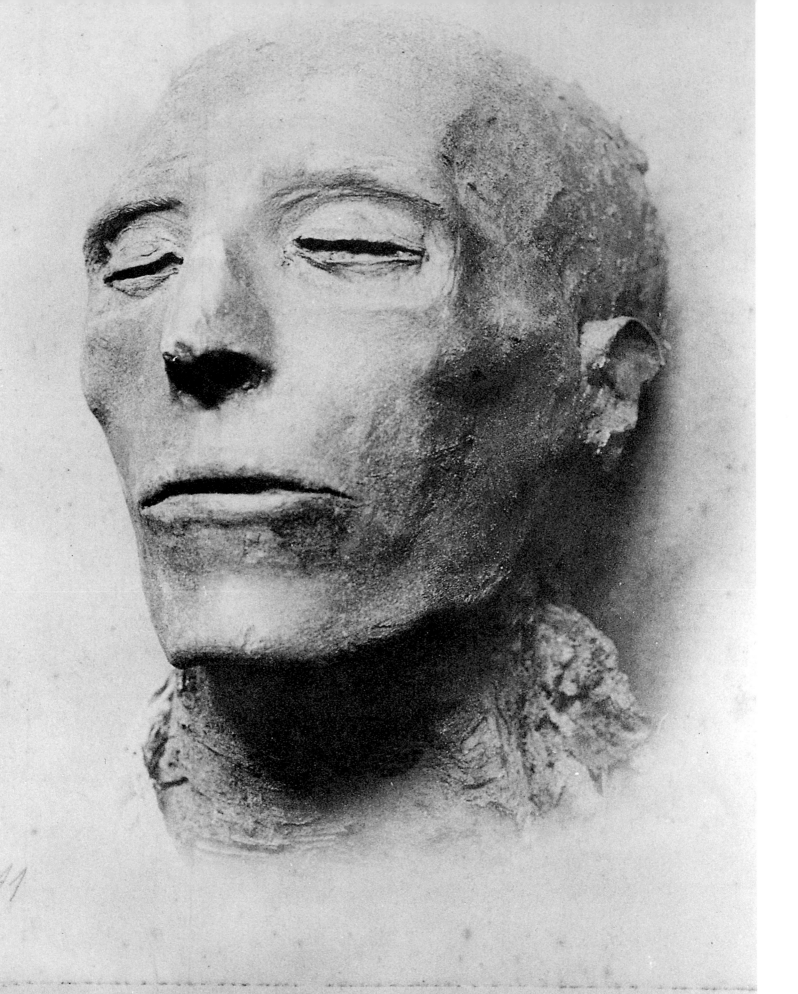

11

Seti I
(19. Dynastie)

III

MODERN RESEARCH INTO MUMMIES

UNTIL THE END OF THE LAST CENTURY, THE ONLY WAY TO examine a mummy was to unwrap it, thereby destroying it in the process. This situation changed radically in 1895 with the discovery of X-rays. Within a year, X-rays were used to view an Egyptian child mummy. With this new technique, it was possible to see inside a mummy without damaging the linen wrappings.

This form of examination was very slow to gain acceptance. On the one hand, museum directors were loathe to allow objects to leave their collections for research purposes. On the other hand, mummies were still associated with fairgrounds and chambers of horrors, and scientists were not keen to have anything to do with mere curios. In

117 Mummy of the Pharaoh Sethos I,
New Kingdom, 19th Dynasty,
photograph by Emil Brugsch, 1886

those days, Egyptologists were not concerned with the age of the person inside the wrappings or with the illnesses they might have suffered from. Their sole interest lay in any amulets and papyri included with the body, and these objects were most easily discovered by simply cutting through the wrappings. The bodies themselves were not considered to possess any scientific interest whatsoever.

On June 27, 1921, Georg Möller, the director of the Ägyptisches Museum, Berlin, sent a circular letter to his colleagues:

Dear Sir,

On Monday July 11th at 10 o'clock a.m., and if necessary the following day too, in the Egyptian Section, we shall be unwrapping a simple 22nd Dynasty mummy from our older collection. We are informing you of this should you happen to be in the area and like to be present.

At least Möller was proposing to spend a whole day or more on unwrapping the mummy, in contrast to the fifteen minutes it had taken in Cairo in 1886 to cut through the wrappings of the mummy of Ramesses II!

Interdisciplinary collaboration with scientists for the purposes of research into mummies only developed very gradually. In recent years, however, Egyptologists have become convinced that scientific methods are extremely useful in providing additional information on the culture and environmental and living conditions of ancient Egypt.

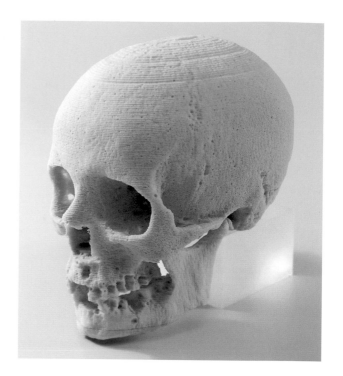

THE POTENTIAL OF X-RAY TECHNOLOGY — FACIAL RECONSTRUCTION

FROM THE WALLS OF TEMPLES AND TOMBS THEY LOOK down at us, the smooth faces of the ancient Egyptians. The visitor wanders, fascinated, from one scene to the next — moments from everyday life, religious activities, depictions of the afterlife. Yet the participants in these scenes remain at a certain distance, because all of them, even the statues, are represented as idealised images of humanity, in the fashion of the day. As in the case of funerary masks, reliefs and wall-paintings almost never reflect people's actual appearance. Differences in style mark out works as belonging to particular periods and distinguish one pharaoh from another, but it is only very rarely that we are confronted with a distinctly individual human being.

Furthermore, while it is true that the sophistication of the art of embalming during the New Kingdom has preserved for us the features of one or two individual pharaohs (cf. illus. 117), in most cases — as a result of the process of mummification and wrapping, or due to damage wrought by grave robbers — the features have been altered to such an extent that it is impossible for us to draw any real conclusions from the mummy itself about a person's appearance in life.

Opposite page

118   Mummy of a woman in the lower part of a coffin,

Ptolemaic, c. 300 B.C.

Length: 150 cms.

From Akhmim. Kestner-Museum, Hanover,

Inv. LMH 7849

119   Synthetic model of the skull of the wrapped

female mummy, made by Medizinelektronik GmbH, Kiel.

Kestner-Museum, Hanover

120   Facial reconstruction of the mummy, reconstructed and

modelled by Richard Helmer, Bonn, and the make-up artist,

Frank Mohr, Hamburg.

Kestner-Museum, Hanover

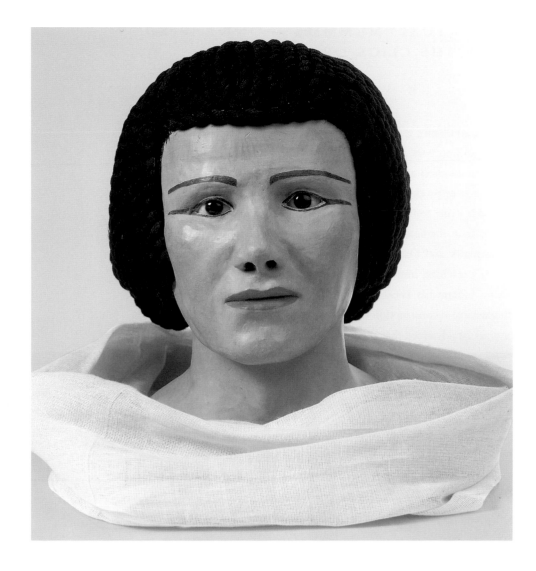

So how can we discover what the ancient Egyptians really looked like? Nowadays, a sense of reserve inhibits us from opening up a mummy's linen wrappings and exposing the face of someone who died many centuries ago to the curiosity of the present generation. In order, therefore, to find out more without destroying the mummies themselves, a small team of highly specialised scientists came together from various universities. The subject of the investigation was provided by the Kestner-Museum, Hanover: a female mummy lying in her coffin with intact linen wrappings, a cartonnage mask, decorations, and a net of beads (see illus. 118). She had been found in the large burial complex at Akhmim in 1884. The style of painted decorations on the coffin and the case puts the date at around 300 B.C. Twenty-three hundred years after her death, the intention was to use state-of-the-art technology to reconstruct the woman's appearance.

Facial reconstruction according to skull shape has been practiced for some time, particularly in the field of forensic medicine. But in the case of this mummy, the skull was not available for examination. First, it had to be reconstructed. In order to establish the necessary measurements, CT scans were carried at intervals of less than a sixteenth of an inch (1 millimetre). The ensuing mass of data made it possible to calculate the measurements of the skull in three dimensions. This new data was in turn entered into a different computer programme which allows the operator to 'unwrap' the head of the mummy and see 'inside' the skull with no more than the click of a mouse (see p. 118 ff.).

The same data was transferred to a computer-driven moulding machine which then produced an exact synthetic model of the head (see illus. 119). This model was so precise in its detail that it provided enough information for a facial reconstruction (see illus. 120). A wig was made by a make-up artist on the basis of typical Egyptian illustrations of the time.

It is perhaps with mixed feelings that we can now view the reconstruction of the head of this young woman who died sometime between the age of twenty and thirty in the valley of the Nile. Our ideas of how the ancient Egyptians looked have been so strongly influenced by the many idealised images which have come down to us that we may find it hard to relate to this face. With her gilded funerary mask and linen wrappings, this mummy still seems to resist modern technology and will never fully reveal the secret of her personality.

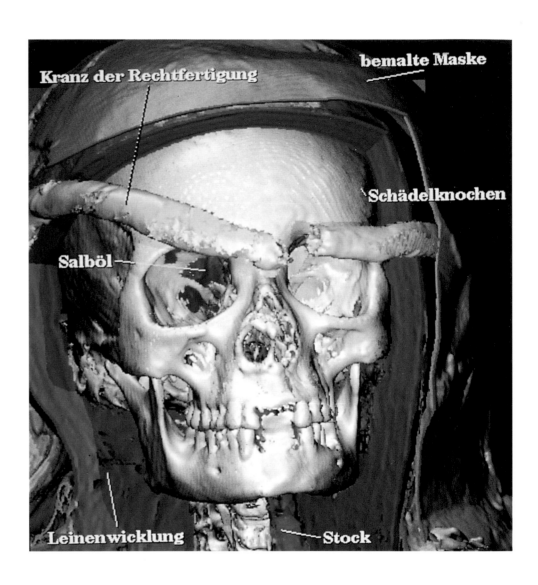

LOOKING A MUMMY IN THE MOUTH

THE ÄGYPTISCHES MUSEUM DER UNIVERSITÄT LEIPZIG HAS a very well-preserved mummy from the Roman period (see illus. 123). The head and chest area are protected by a finely worked cartonnage mask with a gilded face and inlaid eyes of coloured glass. The hair is painted as fine lines falling over the forehead in delicate strands with curled ends. On the hair is a band with *wadjet* amulets; a female vulture painted on the cartonnage spreads her wings protectively behind the deceased's head. On either side of the neck are the goddesses Isis and Nephthys, each in front of yet another deity.

There is a second section of cartonnage on the mummy's body. It is hard to make out the painted decorations because of the narrow crosswise strips of linen, but it is possible to distinguish colourful floral decorations, a winged goddess, and Anubis dispersing incense above the mummy as it lies on its bier.

Before this mummy went to Leipzig, it was in the collection of the Staatliches Museum Schwerin, although there are no records there of how it made the journey from Egypt. Since the Schwerin holdings go back to the art collection of the grand duke of Mecklenburg-Schwerin,

Opposite page

122   Part of the 1996 Hamburg IMDM computer programme.
View into the interior of the mummy. For further information the user simply
clicks on different parts of the image

123   Female mummy with cartonnage mask, 1st century B.C. – 1st century A.D.
Length: 164 cms.
Ägyptisches Museum der Universität Leipzig, Inv. 7813

Overleaf

124   X-ray of the head of the Leipzig mummy, clearly showing
the mask, the skull and the coin

125   Three dimensional reconstruction of the teeth and jaw (side view)

126   CT scan of the head of the mummy

127   Three dimensional reconstruction of the teeth and jaw (frontal view)

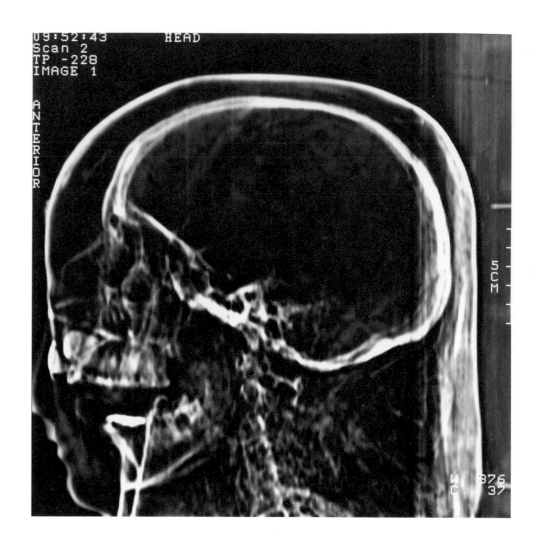

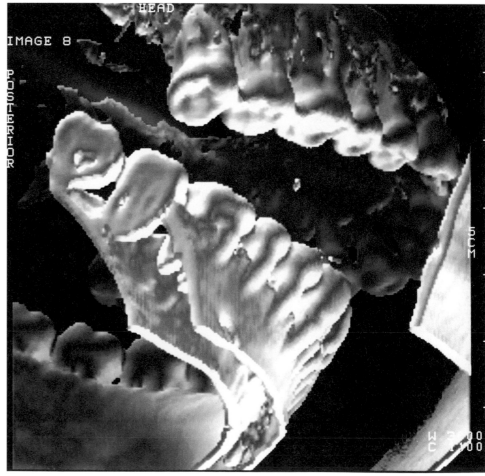

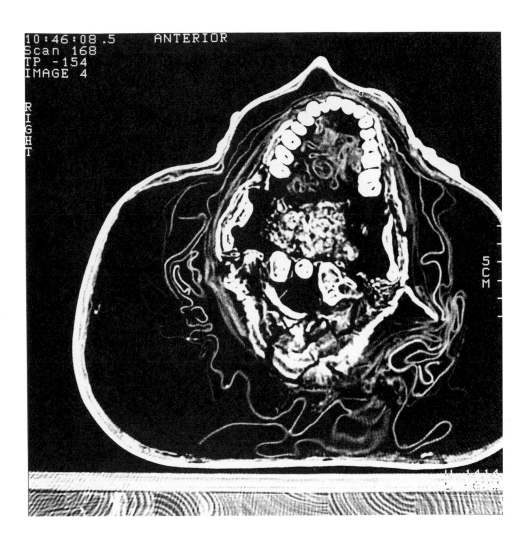

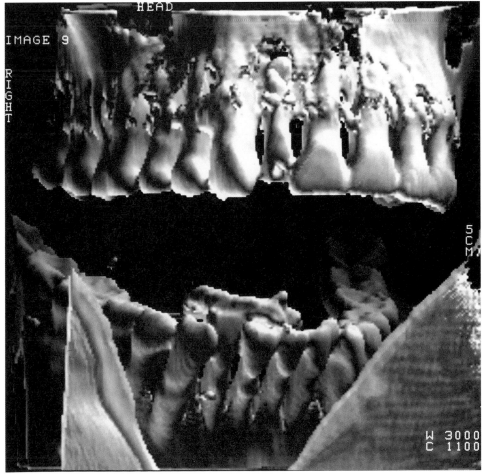

the mummy may well have been acquired at the time of Grand Duke Friedrich-Franz II's Oriental journey in 1872, when he travelled in Egypt with his wife and numerous courtiers. His guide was Heinrich Brugsch, who had also accompanied the Prussian prince Friedrich-Karl on his travels in Egypt. The grand duke also met Heinrich's brother, Emil, the curator and dealer. Since it was through Emil that the town of Hamm had acquired their mummy, it is possible that the mummy now in Leipzig also was obtained through Emil Brugsch.

The Leipzig mummy was recently examined there using the most advanced X-ray techniques. One of the scientists present was a dental practitioner, so the examination concentrated partly on the condition of the mummy's teeth.

Conventional X-rays had already shown that the mummy's mouth was open underneath the linen wrappings; the lower jaw is held in this position either by a wire or by a thread soaked in embalming oils. On the tongue is a metal coin (cf. illus. 124). Placing a coin in the mouth of a deceased person was actually a Greek custom and very rare in Graeco-Roman Egypt. It was meant to be the money used by the deceased to make the journey into the underworld, which means that it had a different religious meaning from the gold tongue pieces that are found more frequently in mummies (see illus. 14). The latter were meant to magically imbue the deceased with the power of speech in the afterlife.

CT scans (see illus. 126) revealed further information about the mouth area of the Leipzig mummy. The embalmers had placed two pads of linen inside the mouth. The piece towards the back had been soaked in embalming oils, as is evident from its greater optical density, which makes it show up lighter on the computer image. The linen towards the front is much looser in comparison. All the teeth of the upper jaw are present. Three-dimensional imaging was used to visualise the mummy's teeth and jaws. Illustration 125 shows a side view of the upper and lower jaw with the teeth and their roots. The grinding surfaces of the teeth in the upper jaw are severely eroded. Illustration 127 was taken looking directly into the mouth and shows the coin behind the lower teeth. These are also very worn. The crown of the right incisor is broken. The bone marrow is exposed by the break running diagonally to the front. The jawbone is absorbed in the root region. This finding makes it clear that the tooth was not broken during the mummification process. It probably broke due to sideways pressure from the other teeth while the jaw was still growing. There is no sign of caries.

128   X-ray of the lumbar veterbrae and sacral region of Ankhhapy

Opposite page

129   The mummy of Ankhhapy, 2nd-1st century B.C.

Length: 155 cms.

Probably from Akhmim.

Pelizaeus-Museum, Hildesheim, Inv. 1905

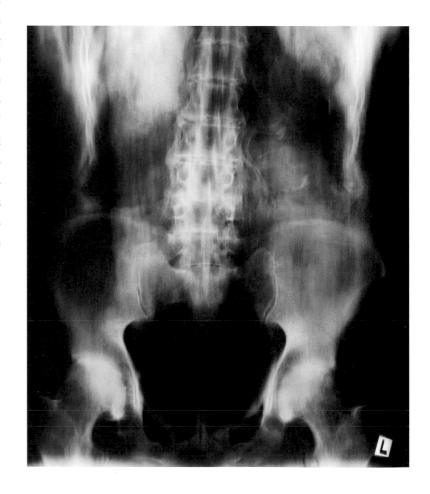

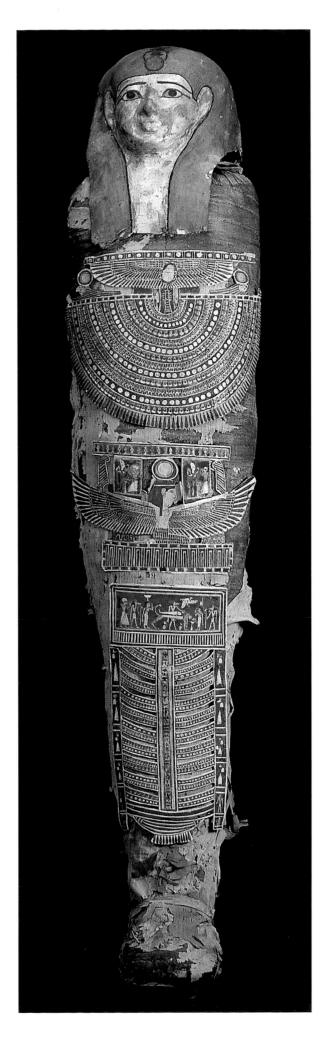

IN 1885, WILHELM PELIZAEUS ACQUIRED A MUMMY AND ITS coffin from a dealer in Cairo. The mummy is now in the Roemer- und Pelizaeus-Museum, Hildesheim (see illus. 129). Nothing was known about its provenance. However, the style of the coffin decoration and the painting on the cartonnage case indicate that the mummy had once been buried in the extensive necropolis of Akhmim in Middle Egypt, one of the largest in ancient Egypt. This was further supported by the inscription on the coffin naming the deceased as Ankhhapy, which translates as 'May the Nile live.' It also names his father, Nesmin, 'He who belongs to (the god) Min'. One of the main cult centres for Min was the temple in Akhmim, and it is likely that Ankhhapy's father carried out the duties of a priest there. The burial of Ankhhapy can be dated at some point during the second or first century B.C.

The mummy's head is covered by a simple cartonnage mask with a gilded face and a blue wig. On the body are three further sections of cartonnage. The breast section has a painted scarab and a colourful collar of flowers. The middle section shows Nut, the goddess of the sky, her wings outspread to protect the mummy. The lower section depicts the mummy lying on a bier with Anubis standing behind it. In the centre of this section of cartonnage, there is an offering prayer inscribed in vertical hieroglyphs. Cartonnage soles are attached below the feet. The linen wrappings have been coloured black to a large extent by the resinous embalming oils.

X-rays revealed the method that had been used to mummify the body. All the organs had been removed from the chest and abdominal cavities. After this, the thorax had been filled with linen. The brain had also been removed and large quantities of resinous embalming oils poured into the skull, forming a crust on the upper surface as they solidified.

The X-rays show the skeleton of a fully grown man. His arms lie crossed over his chest. His age when he died is hard to estimate, but since the bones show no signs of degeneration, he may have been about fifty.

The nails which also show up on the X-rays are not of ancient Egyptian origin. They were used by Egyptian antiquities dealers to secure loose wrappings and have been found in other mummies from the necropolis in Akhmim which were sold at the end of the last century.

One feature which stood out in the X-rays inspired a hunt in other museums for mummies of relatives of Ankhhapy: a deformity of his fifth lumbar vertebra (see illus. 130). The right vertebra had grown into the sacrum below. This condition often leads to neuralgia in the sacral region, and it may be assumed that Ankhhapy suffered from lower back pain. Distortions of this kind, so-called sacralisation, are congenital and can be hereditary in some families. As it turned out, in Liverpool Museum, there is a mummy of a man that also seems to have come from Akhmim and that also shows sacralisation. The decorations on the coffin are painted in the same style as those on Ankhhapy's coffin,

as has already been proven in the case of at least one natural prehistoric mummy. A few years ago, the same test procedures identified malarial illnesses in Egyptian mummies.

Mummies show that the ancient Egyptians were not only attacked internally by parasites, but externally, too. Remains of lice and nits, the larvae of lice, have been found in mummies' hair or caught in the teeth of fine combs (see illus. 132). Lice are not only unpleasant vermin but also spread disease, above all typhus. Since lice only colonise live hair, it seems that the practice amongst the Egyptian élite of shaving their heads and wearing wigs made a lot of sense from the point of view of hygiene.

Examinations of mummies have shown that many Egyptians, including the royal family, had horrifyingly bad teeth. From an early age, there was damage to the grinding surfaces, and by the middle years the enamel was often completely eroded. This resulted in abscesses. The reason that the Egyptians' teeth were so worn was the presence of tiny particles of stone in the flour used to make bread. Tests on bread from that time have even led to the suggestion that sand was intentionally added to the wheat in order to make milling easier. But anyone who has travelled in Egypt and eaten sandwiches in the shade of a temple or pyramid will confirm that this need not have been the case, for sand is everywhere, even in the air, and one can feel it grating on one's teeth while chewing.

Medical papyri describe some remedies for toothache and loose teeth, but these probably cannot have been very effective. No mummy yet has shown signs of dental treatment such as boring or filling. This makes the find dating from the end of the Old Kingdom in a tomb in the state officials' cemetery by the pyramids of Giza all the more astonishing — namely, two lower molars linked together by a piece of gold wire (see illus. 131). When they were found in 1917 by Junker, they were already separated from the jaw, lying loose amongst the bones of a broken skeleton. This find has been widely discussed by dentists, but so far there has been no definitive agreement as to whether these teeth were linked in this way during the deceased's lifetime or were wired together after death.

A second find of this sort consisted of three teeth held together by gold wire, although these do not definitely date from the Old Kingdom. In fact, evidence of this kind of dental work does not re-emerge until two thousand years later in the case of a mummy from the Ptolemaic Period which has two teeth joined by a silver wire in situ in the upper jaw. But this later find is much less surprising, because by that time this use of metal wire to secure loose teeth was current in other Mediterranean countries, too.

Average life expectancy in ancient Egypt was not very high, partly because of the high rate of infant mortality and partly because of the limitations of medical treatment. Numerous mummies show the age at the time of death to have been between thirty and forty. And yet, there were some who did reach the biblical 'three score and ten', as the following tomb inscription shows: 'I spent 77 years, nine months and 20 days in which I honoured the eternal pharaoh.'

132 A mummy's hair with a wooden comb, New Kingdom. Rijksmuseum van Oudheden, Leiden, Inv. 1942/9.8

MUMMIES BEAR WITNESS
TO THEIR OWN TIME

DESPITE THEIR PAINSTAKING PREPARATIONS, MOST ANCIENT Egyptians did not fulfil their desire for eternal life, inextricably linked as it was with the preservation of the body, for countless mummies were already destroyed by their descendants to make way for the next generation. Then in modern times, Europeans collected mummies to grind them into powder for medicines and painters' dyes and to make paper out of the linen wrappings. Contemporary researchers are doing their best to keep the ancient Egyptians alive by allowing no further destruction. Now, we have our own ceremonies of the Opening of the Mouth that let the mummies bear witness to their times, to life in pharaonic Egypt and even to their own fate as individuals.

THE RESTORATION AND CONSERVATION
OF A CARTONNAGE CASE

Jens Klocke

The mummy case to be examined here was made for the burial of an Egyptian who seems to have lived in the Fayum Oasis almost two thousand years ago, when Egypt was already a Roman province. It is not known when the sanctity of his tomb was disturbed, but it was towards the end of the nineteenth century that this case finally arrived in the relatively new Museum für Kunst und Gewerbe, Hamburg. Since nothing was known about this item beyond its original inventory card, the restorer had to carry out detailed examinations of the object and consult the relevant literature to gather the information necessary to decide how to proceed with the restoration process.

133   Mummy's cartonnage mask, after restoration.
Museum für Kunst und Gewerbe Hamburg

STRUCTURE AND PRODUCTION

THE FRAMEWORK OF THIS SO-CALLED CARTONNAGE CASE IS four to six layers of coarse linen, which were stuck together by means of animal sizing to a base of clay and straw. This base is evident today from just one tiny piece of straw that was originally hidden under painted decorations, but that now shows on the linen where the paint has come away.

The layers of linen are covered with a coating of sized chalk, which was also used to model the face and ears. When this was still wet, it was easy enough to put the glass inlays for the eyes in position. After this, the case was gilded and decorated using water-soluble paints bound with gum arabic.

During the restoration work, the question arose as to why the funerary mask of a North African should gaze out at us with glowing green eyes. Could this be evidence of some early northern European influence? By chance, the riddle was solved when some moisture seeped between the lens and the white glass during cleaning, and for a brief moment the iris turned deep brown, as it must once have been. The adhesive used to set the transparent lenses into the white glass had become dry and brittle, with the result that there had been a change in its refractive properties, causing black-brown eyes to become green.

MEDITERRANEAN SEA

0   200 miles

0   300 km

⊙ ALEXANDRIA   TANIS ⊙
           ⊙ QANTIR

L O W E R   E G Y P T

MERIMDE ⊙   ⊙ HELIOPOLIS

GIZA ⊙   ● CAIRO
ABUSIR ⊙
SAQQARA ⊙   ⊙ MEMPHIS
DAHSHUR ⊙
        ⊙ LISHT
FAIYUM ⊙
        ⊙ EL HIBE

NILE

⊙ BENI HASSAN
HERMOPOLIS ⊙
      ⊙ AMARNA
MEIR ⊙
     ⊙ DEIR EL-GEBRAWI
ASSIUT ⊙
     ⊙ QAU
AKHMIM ⊙

           ● QUFT
ABYDOS ⊙   ⊙ KOPTOS
    NAQADA ⊙   ● QUS
DEIR EL-MEDINA ⊙
      ⊙ LUXOR/THEBES

E G Y P T

U P P E R   E G Y P T

HIERAKONPOLIS ⊙

FIRST CATARACT   ⊙ KOM OMBO

ELEPHANTINE ⊙   ● ASWAN
       ⊙ PHILAE

L O W E R   N U B I A   LAKE NASSER

R E D   S E A

CHRONOLOGY

PREHISTORIC PERIOD

until 3000 B.C.
The dead are wrapped in animal skins or mats and buried in the desert sand. Wind and heat dry them out, forming 'natural mummies'.

EARLY DYNASTIC PERIOD

1st and 2nd Dynasties, 2925–2857 B.C.
Egypt develops into a nation-state through the gradual amalgamation of various different areas.
The bodies of the dead are wrapped in strips of linen.

OLD KINGDOM

3rd Dynasty, 2657–2581 B.C.
Egyptian culture in the ascendant. The Step-Pyramid at Saqqara is built.

4th Dynasty, 2581–2466 B.C.
Construction of the mighty pyramids at Giza.
First attempts at mummifying the dead. Canopic jars containing wrapped viscera are placed in the tombs of royal personnages.

5th Dynasty, 2466–2325 B.C.
First high point in the cult of the sun-god, Ra. Sun-temples built.
Officials of the state become increasingly powerful and build extensive tombs for themselves. Tomb furnishings now usually include four canopic jars. Bodies are skilfully wrapped in order to give them as lifelike an appearance as possible.

6th Dynasty, 2325–2154 B.C.
The dissolution of central government.

FIRST INTERMEDIATE PERIOD

8th until the first half of the 11th Dynasty, 2154–2030 B.C.
Internal chaos results from rapid changes of rulers and rivalry to gain control of the throne.

MIDDLE KINGDOM

Reunification of Egypt until the end of the 11th Dynasty, 2030–1994 B.C.; 12th Dynasty, 1994–1781 B.C.
Egypt becomes a major power in the eastern Mediterranean area. The royal residence is at Memphis, and the religious centre is at Thebes.
Techniques of mummification are honed through constant experiment.

SECOND INTERMEDIATE PERIOD

13th to 17th Dynasties, 1781–1542 B.C.
Egypt is ruled after 1650 B.C. by the Hyksos from northern Asia.

NEW KINGDOM

18th Dynasty, 1542–1305 B.C.
Revival of Egypt's dominance in the region. Intensive contacts with northern Asia. Attempts under Amenhotep IV/Akhenaten to establish a monotheistic sun-religion. The royal residence moves for a short period to El-Amarna. The old order is reinstated at the end of the dynasty.
Mummification becomes more refined than ever before.

19th Dynasty, 1305–1189 B.C.
Growing influence of the militia on internal politics.
In tomb decorations representations of the underworld become increasingly important.